ANN LOUISE GITTLEMAN'S

EAT FAT, LOSE WEIGHT
COOKBOOK

Also by Ann Louise Gittleman, N.D., C.N.S.

ANN LOUISE GITTLEMAN'S
EAT FAT, LOSE WEIGHT COOKBOOK

Ann Louise Gittleman, N.D., C.N.S.

with

Ann Castro and Claudia Galofre Krevat

KEATS PUBLISHING

LOS ANGELES

NTC/Contemporary Publishing Group

Library of Congress Cataloging-in-Publication Data

Gittleman, Ann Louise.
    [Eat fat, lose weight cookbook}
    Ann Louise Gittleman's eat fat, lose weight cookbook / Ann Louise Gittleman with
Ann Castro and Claudia Galofre Krevat.
        p.   cm.
    Includes bibliographical references and index.
    ISBN 0-658-01220-7
    1. Reducing diets—Recipes. 2. Omega-3 fatty acids. 3. Omega-6 fatty acids.
    4. Fatty acids in human nutrition. I. Castro, Ann. II. Krevat, Claudia Galofre. III. Title.
    RM222.2 .G537 2001
    613.s'5—dc21

                                                                    00-051462

Published by Keats, a division of
NTC/Contemporary Publishing Group, Inc.
4255 West Touhy Avenue
Lincolnwood, Illinois 60712, U.S.A.

01 02 03 04 DHD 18 17 16 15 14 13 12 11 10 9 8 7 6 5 4 3 2 1

International Standard Book Number: 0-658-01220-7

This book was set in Adobe Garamond by Nancy Freeborn.
Interior design by Nancy Freeborn

Printed and bound by RR. Donnelley & Sons Co.

TO MARIA LOW,
OUR KITCHEN ANGEL

Contents

Acknowledgments

I offer my heartfelt thanks and unconditional appreciation to the following individuals for their steadfast support, culinary assistance, and creativity:

- First and foremost to Ann Castro, my right-hand collaborator, who has the uncanny gift of being able to portray what's in my mind through the written word, even before I have expressed my thoughts to her. Her wonderful writing ability as well as cooking expertise has immeasurably contributed to the flavor of this book. I will be eternally grateful to her not just for her consummate professionalism but also for her willingness to jump right into this project at the eleventh hour.

- To Philomena Consiglio (Ann Castro's beautiful mother) and her sister Andrea Snowden, son Jason Martin, and loyal (and charming) husband Oscar Castro, who shared many of their family favorites with us. They also doubled as recipe tasters along with Ann's nephews Matt Snowden and Brian Snowden, and Evelyn Gaona (Jason's lifelong partner).

- To Claudia Krevat, for her enticingly delicious recipes, which constitute a sizable portion of this cookbook. To Steve Krevat (Claudia's husband) and daughter Gabriella for their continuous support and encouragement. Also to Mamaeso, Claudia's live-in family cook when she was growing up in South America. Mamaeso taught Claudia that the main ingredient in cooking was love.

- To Caroline Pincus, book midwife and my former editor at Harper San Francisco, for her insightful, consulting services.

- To the entire staff at NTC/Contemporary Publishing Group, who were so enthusiastic about this project: Peter Hoffman, executive editor at Keats; Jack Artenstein, managing director and publisher at Keats; Claudia McCowan, editor; Jama Cartrer, managing editor; Carmela Carvajal, project editor; Robin Lockwood, publicity director; John Nolan, publisher (and a wonderfully accessible publisher at that); Greg Euson; Neal McNish; Robert Lombardi; Linda Babat; and Phyllis Herman, nutritionist, editor, and writer, for her painstaking editing and proofreading talents on behalf of Keats.

- To the entire ALG Inc. group, who helped keep my affairs flowing smoothly while I was in my creative mode. But especially to Stuart Gittleman, whose wit, charm, and managerial know-how were essential factors in keeping me on track. Thank you to Arthur Gittleman; Bob Mitchell; Judy Straayer; Steve Kambourian; and Renee Chernus for providing your business acumen and legal expertise.

- To Laura Tengelsen, my summer of 2000 nutrition intern, for her willing recipe testing and loving spirit. To Krystie Gummer, my trusty administrative assistant and personal secretary, for her careful review of this manuscript and carb counting.

- To my teachers, mentors, and fellow professionals whom I honor and admire: Robert Akins, M.D.; Elson Hass, M.D.; Ronald Hoffman, M.D.; Stephen Sinatra, M.D.; Leo Frangipane, M.D.; Julian Whitaker, M.D.; Jonathan Wright, M.D.; John Lee, M.D.; Joseph Mercola, D.O.; Charles Wharton, Ph.D.; Uzzi Reiss, M.D.; Nan Fuchs, Ph.D.; Hyla Cass, M.D.; Ilena Rosenthal; Marty Zucker; D. Lindsay Berkson, Ph.D.; Joseph Dispenza; Joanie Greggains; Bonnie Coleen; Jack Tipps, N.D.; and David Essel—"Mr. Positive!"

- To the many journalists, editors, and marketing directors who have spread my nutritional messages throughout the world: Beth Salmon, Olivia Bell Buehl, Brenda Kearns, Jan Sheehan, Linda Giuca, Barbara Tunick, Noreen Flanagan, Roon Frost, Lyle Hurd, Kelly James-Enger, Erica Jorgensen, Patricia King Siri Khalsa, Rhody Lake, Tony Presutto, Bill Sardi, Barrie-Louise Switzen, Gailon Totheroh, Nigel J. and Patricia Yorwerth, Nina Likins, Mike Danielson, Simon Gook, and L. A. Justice.

- To the public relations firms and individuals who have valiantly represented me throughout my career: Hill Knowlton; Barston Marstellar; Annie Jennings (a wonderful human being as well as a great publicist); Karen Villanueva (a diligent and highly resourceful PR dynamo); and Gerald McGlothlin and Carla Rajca, who have become my friends.

- To all of my Web friends, especially: the ivillage.com/diet/boards' ladies and gentlemen who communicate with me daily; Allison Rand, Meredith Leo, Emily Lapkin, and Rebecca Taylor; the NutriNews.com gang, especially Richard Enlow, Barry Hays, Jerry Freeman, Jim Townsend, and Don Templet; and the myprimetime.com group, especially Kerri Brenner and Marjorie McAneny.

- To my circle of caregivers and personal healers: Dr. Roy Speiser; Dr. Diane Romeo; Dr. Ronald Hecht; Dr. Greg Hoell; Dr. Merle Bouma; Dr. Olga

Klebanova; Dr. Thomas Nybo; Dr. Ron Davis; Noel Clark; Yvette Moore; Mary Ann Alexander; the Grannies; Georgia Cold; and Vickie Killion, my magnificent wardrobe consultant whose energy and flair keep me in style.

- To my lifelong family of friends, who were so enthralled with the idea of a cookbook that I couldn't let them down: Linda Hooper, John Desgrey, Elizabeth and Monroe Krichman, Dianna and Dick Fredrick, Helen and Bill Malm, and Ann Oliphant.

- To my precious nephews Isaac Aaron Gittleman and Daniel Ryan Gittleman, my niece Shira Beth Gittleman, and my "surrogate" daughter Carol Faye Templeton, who make all of this worthwhile.

- To my mother, Edith Gittleman, whoase famous recipes are incorporated herein. My mother is not only a wonderful cook and exemplary mother but is also a gifted leader in her own right. Her talents are greatly admired and appreciated by the other women of Hadassah, the Beth Israel religious school community, and her family. We love you Ma!

- And, of course, as always, to Boo Boo.

CHAPTER ONE

GETTING STARTED

Welcome Fat Back!

Avocados . . . walnuts . . . almonds . . . pumpkin seeds . . . sesame seeds . . . salmon . . . olive oil. Wouldn't you love to start eating these "forbidden" foods again, and get off the dieting merry-go-round once and for all? Well, you can—and actually *lose* weight while you're doing it.

The *Eat Fat, Lose Weight Cookbook* helps you say farewell to the cuisine of deprivation, and introduces you to a whole new cuisine of celebration. You'll develop a brand-new attitude toward eating, one that focuses on the amazing omega fats—fats that not only brim with flavor, but which are bursting with health benefits. Besides revving up your metabolism to help you lose weight, omega fats have been shown in numerous studies to help lower the risk of heart attacks, Alzheimer's disease, arthritis, breast cancer, and even menstrual irregularities from PMS to perimenopause and beyond.

Let's be honest: The no- or low-fat, high-carbohydrate diet highly popular during the last twenty years has failed miserably. In fact, in the past two decades, Americans have become even fatter; today a whopping 55 percent of adults are at least 20 pounds overweight. Along with this massive weight gain, the incidence of Type 2 diabetes has skyrocketed in the past thirty years. Moreover, the low-fat, high-carb diet has had virtually no effect on the prevalence of heart disease.

Culture Clues

The truth is, the trimmest and healthiest people throughout the world follow eating programs that are far from fat free. Take a look at the Greeks, Turks, Italians, French, or Spanish, for instance. Their Mediterranean diet—rich in the omega oils—is actually considered to be the world's healthiest cuisine. And yet it is full of olive oil, seeds, nuts, and fatty fish (such as sardines), as well as fresh, colorful fruits and vegetables. Even though they consume a diet that contains 40 percent fat, these populations are slim and boast the lowest rates of heart disease in the world.

Omega-rich foods are also found in Asian cuisine with its sumptuous fish (such as salmon and mackerel) and flavorful fats (such as peanut oil). As a matter of fact, studies in Japan have even linked the omega oils from fatty fish such as anchovies and salmon to a lowered rate of depression. Likewise, Middle Eastern dishes are full of omegas, from sesame seeds and tahini (sesame seed paste) to olive oil. Many of the Latin dishes we find so tantalizing use omega-rich ingredients such as avocado in salsas, dips, and salads. And in the Caribbean, peanuts, another omega-rich food, are a special choice ingredient in numerous ethnic dishes. Nuts—such as cashews, pine nuts, walnuts, and pecans—are longtime global favorites, used in various items from baked goods and garnishes to condiments for poultry, meat, and lamb dishes.

Clearly, it's not the amount of fat but the type of fat that counts. And that's what this *Eat Fat, Lose Weight Cookbook* is all about—eating the right kinds of fats from the omega-3, omega-6, and omega-9 families.

The Omega Star Weight-Loss Players

Omega-3s: Crucial to Weight Loss. Omega-3 fats help your body to burn fat efficiently. They boost your natural fat-burning ability by increasing the production of tissuelike hormones known as eicosanoids, which stimulate the body's ability to burn fat rather than storing it. In addition, since the omega-3s are polyunsaturated fats, their biochemical structure easily permeates cellular walls, producing satiety and inhibiting overeating.

Moreover, omega-3 fats are a necessary ingredient for balanced brain function; as such, they provide a real help for problems such as attention deficit hyperactivity disorder (ADHD). Omega-3s also prevent blood clotting, repair tissue damage caused by clogged arteries, lower triglycerides and high blood pressure, and protect the body from autoimmune diseases such as rheumatoid arthritis.

These delectable oils are found in fatty fish such as salmon, mackerel, trout, anchovies, and sardines. They're also found in flaxseeds and flaxseed oil as well as walnuts, Brazil nuts (also high in selenium), and pumpkin seeds. Both flaxseed meal and flaxseeds lead the pack as the highest sources of omega-3s—which is why you'll find some creative uses for them on pages 151 to 156 in our section geared for kids called Tasty Treats. We've made it a point to offer desserts so delicious, kids won't even realize that they're nutritious. And since the recipes are rich in omega-3s, they help calm down hyperactive kids at the same time by fortifying the brain with essential nutrients.

Omega-6s: Fat Burners, Par Excellence. From sunflower seeds, pine nuts, and pistachios to evening primrose oil and borage oil supplements, omega-6s are outstanding for firing up metabolism to moisturize dry skin, nourish listless hair, and strengthen brittle nails. Taken as a concentrated dietary supplement called conjugated linoleic acid (CLA), omega-6s prompt the body to burn stored fat as energy, resulting in a decrease in body fat and a proportional increase in muscle tissue, which in turn burns even more calories.

Omega-9s: The Heart-Smart Fats. Omega-9s help lower cholesterol, reduce the risk of heart attack, and protect arteries. Some studies of Italian women suggest that olive oil (rich in omega-9s) can prevent breast cancer. Other vital sources of omega-9s are avocados, sesame seeds, peanuts, cashews, hazelnuts, macadamias, and almonds.

But the best news for food lovers everywhere is that the omega family of fats provides long-term appetite satisfaction so that you stay filled up longer. With the right amounts of omegas in the diet, you will be content with less food and not be tempted to overeat. Putting crunchy nuts, roasted seeds, fresh fish, and olive oil–rich salad dressing back into your menu plans will keep you satisfied for hours, not just for fifteen minutes. After all, it's the oils and fats that are the real flavor carriers of food, giving us sustained eating pleasure.

The Eat Fat, Lose Weight *Promise*

Readers who have faithfully followed the advice in the predecessor to this cookbook, *Eat Fat, Lose Weight* (Keats, 1999), have lost more than 10 pounds in three weeks simply by adding back the essential healthy fats into their meals, with a satisfying 30 percent of total calories from fat. Since many of you wanted actual recipes and more expansive menu plans, this cookbook offers quick cuisine ideas tailored to busy lifestyles, with a wide array of delicious dishes to enhance your repertoire. For those of you who have mastered *Eat Fat, Lose Weight,* you will be surprised at the variety of new ethnic ingredients in the shopping list that reflect the book's philosophy. You'll find intriguing touches of formerly forbidden ingredients such as shredded coconut and coconut milk. Although coconut milk may be high in saturated fats, it also happens to be a potent superfood because it is antiviral, antifungal, and antimicrobial. So we use this superstar in moderation to tap into its many health benefits and embellish the taste of our delicious recipes. As a matter of fact, you're going to be seeing both coconut oil and palm oil making a major comeback in this country before too long. Despite their high saturated fat content, these tropical oils possess strong protective qualities. Palm oil, for example, is the most concentrated source of a nutrient known as tocotrienols, a member of the vitamin E family. Palm-based tocotrienols have been found to lower cholesterol, prevent clot formation, regress atherosclerotic plaques, and inhibit the growth of cancer cells.

Undoubtedly, the robust flavors and heady aromas of the *Eat Fat, Lose Weight* cuisine will delight your palate. You will fill up on colorful, nutrient-rich veggies, quality proteins, and a moderate amount of fruit. This slimming plan is also perfect for those opting for a low-carbohydrate diet. If you are watching your carb intake, pay attention to recipes bearing an asterisk (*). These dishes contain 10 or more grams of carbohydrate in the form of grains, legumes, beans, or fruit. Simply adjust the rest of your carbohydrate intake for the day accordingly.

The dietary lifestyle plan outlined in this cookbook will be the *only* eating program you will ever need—guaranteed. By following the easy recipes and sample meal plans, you will look great, feel terrific, and watch the pounds melt away. And since the plan isn't low in fat, you won't feel deprived, which means there's no more fatigue, food cravings, or mood swings. This healthy diet is great for every member of your family, especially kids who may need a little calming down. So get ready to *Eat Fat, Lose Weight* because the new you is only pages away.

How to Use This Book

This cookbook is all about putting the pleasure back into eating by following the basic principles of the *Eat Fat, Lose Weight* philosophy. And it's not difficult, or filled with unappealing foods. Five easy helpers will get you on the weight-loss track . . . fast.

1. *Let's Go Shopping.* First, we'll take you on a shopping trip to the local grocery store or market so you can stock your fridge, freezer, and pantry with the essential ingredients. It all begins on page 9.

2. *The Master Diet Blueprint.* Next, we'll introduce you to an easy, ten-step blueprint so you can create your own plan, based on your individual tastes. (If you're serious about shedding those unwanted pounds and feeling energetic and radiant, then be sure to faithfully follow this master blueprint for success, which is featured on pages 13 to 19.)

3. *Twenty-One-Day Menu Plan.* Then we give you some delicious ideas on pages 21 to 34 for how to make it all work, simply and effortlessly, every day of the week.

4. *"Omegasizing" Your Meals.* You'll want to refer often to this section—which begins on page 35—with its smart tips on how to fortify your recipes using omega-3–rich flaxseed.

5. *The Fat Zappers.* A helpful list of the best supplements is listed on pages 39 to 41 to augment your slimming-down process.

That's all it takes to begin experiencing the *Eat Fat, Lose Weight* momentum sweeping the country. If you don't have to lose weight, but want to nourish your body with healthy fats, this plan is still for you. Just go ahead and delve right into the recipe section. It is surprisingly easy.

Color Me Healthy

What makes this cookbook different from all others is that each meal contains a source of essential, healthy fat. Taking full advantage of the taste and health benefits of the amazing omega foods, we created new recipes as well as put a fun twist on some old-time favorites. These recipes include delicious and healthy sources of fat such as olive oil, tahini, sesame seeds, salmon, avocados, peanut butter, and plenty of nuts, as well as utilizing dark green, leafy veggies.

Both nuts and a rainbow of vegetables have a definite purpose in the *Eat Fat, Lose Weight* plan. That's because hundreds of studies have demonstrated their health benefits. In 1992, researchers analyzed the diets of 31,000 Seventh Day Adventists in California. These individuals, who consumed peanuts or other nuts at least five times per week, had 50 percent less heart disease than those who rarely ate nuts. The Harvard Nurse's Health Study published similar results from research conducted on Iowa women.

Phytonutrients, the potent healing compounds in vegetables, have also been shown in study after study to provide vital support in combating potential risks on several levels by tricking cancer cells. This deceptive maneuver works because the structure of phytonutrients mimics that of cancer-fueling hormones such as estrogen. The dark leafy greens are rich in antioxidants and lutein, which help neutralize the free radicals that damage cells. Citrus peels contain limonoids, phytonutrients that help stir up enzymatic activity to detoxify cancer and have demonstrated an ability to halt or diminish breast tumor growth. Yellowish orange veggies are packed with flavonoids and carotenoids, which contain alpha carotene, beta carotene, lutein, and lycopene to further help suppress cancer potential.

Carotenoids—such as lycopene, a red pigment found in tomatoes—are also known to aid in the reduction of lung and stomach cancer, offering antioxidant protection. Tomatoes and products containing tomatoes have been shown to actually lower the potential for cancer, according to the National Cancer Institute. (For more information on this superstar phytonutrient, be sure to visit lycored.com.)

Needless to say, the link between good nutrition and vibrant health is critical. The scientific community has even hopped on the bandwagon. Scientists are busy bioengineering vegetables and fruits to vastly increase their health-promoting potential. Already available in markets across the nation is the new Zespri Gold kiwi fruit, which is loaded with 120 mg of vitamin C to help combat colds and cancer-inducing free radicals. In Texas, a maroon carrot is being marketed in which the vegetable's beta-carotene qualities are bolstered by 40 percent. The new carrot will be sold nationwide in the next couple of years along with three other potentially great superfoods: a new cherry tomato with ten times the lycopene; a cantaloupe produced in clay soil touting 500 percent higher beta carotene, providing superior vision support; and an innovative broccoli from USDA researchers with three times more of the phytochemical sulforaphane to help thwart the ravages of carcinogenic activity.

To make even more use of the many health-supporting benefits found in foods, practically every tantalizing *Eat Fat, Lose Weight* dish is enhanced with culinary herbs, such as basil, parsley, oregano, dill, garlic, rosemary, cayenne, or cumin. Many of these spices have antiviral properties and contain antioxidants as well as supportive minerals such as potassium, calcium, and iron. Don't miss the Thai recipe (Coco-Nutty Shrimp) on page 131 that features a wonderful seasoning called fish sauce, an interesting blend of omega-rich anchovies and sea salt. A little bit of its concentrated taste goes a long way because the seasoning is also high in sodium. (Those watching blood pressure or having fluid-retention problems should use this sparingly.) We've also carefully blended some of the other non-Asian recipes with sardines and anchovies. For example, the Party Pâté on page 65 is a mouthwatering combination of salmon, anchovies, and smoked oysters. This delectable medley is so subtle that no one would ever guess anchovies are part of the ingredient list!

Introducing the Recipes

The *Eat Fat, Lose Weight* program is more than a clinical one-time diet plan. You will love the delicious meals—not to mention the guaranteed weight-loss results. From the phytonutrients and fiber to the good fats and balanced protein, you'll enjoy a totally new lifestyle for everlasting health.

The good news is that you can start right now by incorporating a few changes into your current eating habits. For example, if the concept of eating fat makes you a little uneasy (even though they are the *healthy fats* from the omega family of fats), then start slowly. Begin by looking through the following recipe sections and choose a dish from each one; pick a starter, soup, salad, entrée, and dessert. Then incorporate one dish at a time into your regular menus. Let your taste buds take over. You've got plenty of delectable recipes to choose from, each one created with the busy family in mind. You might want to make a little extra of your favorites to take to work for lunch the next day.

- **Breakfast** is definitely your chance to start things off nutritionally right. There are a number of refreshing, quick-to-fix smoothies, starting on page 44. For those days when you have a little more time (like on the weekends), there are scrumptious Blueberry Yogurt Flaxjacks, Oatmeal Flax Muffins, and Korny Muffins, as well as a Rainbow Veggie Omelet, One-Two-Three Huevos Rancheros, and a Green Goddess Frittata just aiming to please.

- **Sensational Starters** are an easy way to slip those omegas into your family's dietary routine, featured on pages 58 to 74. You'll be surprised at how easy it is to prepare such crowd-pleasers as Avocado-Cilantro Dip, Tangy Tapenade, Caribbean Hummus, Omega Star Pesto, Paradise Salsa, and Hotsy-Totsy Shrimp Cocktail.

- **Savory Soups and Stupendous Stews,** for which recipes start on page 74, will also be a big hit with your family and friends. Make some ahead and have a bowl for lunch or a light dinner with a side salad. There are the all-time favorites soups such as Hearty Chicken Vegetable and Mushroom Barley as well as specialty soups and stews such as Curried Carrot, Velvety Borscht, and Veal Stew.

- **Main-Dish Salads and Dressings** are great for those lazy spring and summer days. On pages 90 to 103, you'll find a number of interesting creations to whet any appetite; for instance, Sunny Caesar Salad, Mango Salmon Salad, and South Sea Crab Salad. Also included are oh-so-delicious dressings such as Lime-Cilantro, Pepita Plum, and Templeton's Best.

- **Vibrant Vegetables,** starting on page 103, can easily become the perfect accompaniment to any meal, as a side dish or a salad. Try Nutty Broccoli-Cauliflower Salad, Saucy Red Cabbage, Roasted Summer Delight, or Spicy Eggplant.

- **Succulent Seafood** bursts with the amazing omegas, and you'll find a wonderful selection starting on page 118. Enjoy Simply Smashing Snapper, Coconut Salmon, Scallop Rhapsody, Crab Cake Casserole, Coco-Nutty Shrimp, and Outrageous Tuna Burgers.

- **Meats and Poultry** turn ho-hum meals into incredible events. Beginning on page 134, you'll find such delicious choices as Southwest Salisbury Steaks, Mama's Meatloaf, Crunchy Baked Chicken, Cuban-Style Turkey Breast, and Three-Step Veal Cutlets.

- **Tasty Treats** are what kids clamor for—so give them our healthy omega alternatives, beginning on page 151. They won't even know the treats are good for them. Let them crunch on Peanut Butter Balls or Flax Snax Balls, or enjoy a creamy dessert like Yummy-in-Your-Tummy Pudding.

CHAPTER TWO

LET'S GO SHOPPING

Many of the foods on this shopping list can be found in the grocery store, while others (such as flaxseed oil, flaxseed meal, and specialty sweeteners such as stevia) are available in your health food store. Many grocery chains, however, now offer a health section that carries some of these items. In most cases, brand names are included for your shopping convenience. These are the brands we personally use in our kitchen. That does not mean they are the only quality ones available, though.

You'll also notice that the *Eat Fat, Lose Weight* shopping list scales back on refined, white flour–carbohydrate foods such as breads, pastas, and cereals. Many of these foods are processed and vital nutrients have been removed. Instead, you will find lots of colorful and crisp phytochemical-rich vegetables, fruits, and whole grains taking the place of those old starchy standbys.

Here's what you will need to stock the *Eat Fat, Lose Weight* fridge, freezer, and pantry to get you headed toward a slimmer, healthier figure.

The *Eat Fat, Lose Weight* Fridge

- **Oils:** Flaxseed oil, Barleans Essential Woman Oil (a combination of flaxseed oil and evening primrose oil), sesame oil, toasted sesame oil, peanut oil, walnut oil, hazelnut oil

    HELPFUL HINTS: If you live in a northern, cold climate, oils can also be stored in a cool, dark place rather than the fridge. Flaxseed oil is subject to oxidation and is sensitive to air, heat, and light and should only be used in no-heat recipes. Flaxseed oil in 8-ounce containers should be used up in about three weeks. Flax whole or milled can be used for baking, however, since it is more stable. Be sure to read the "Omegasizing" Your Meals section (page 35) for helpful ways to work with flax, including how to make deliciously healthy flax butter and flax tea.

- **Seeds, nuts, and nut butters:** EFAsense Certified Organic Milled Flaxseed, sesame seeds, pumpkin seeds, raw almonds, hazelnuts, pecans, walnuts, peanuts, cashews, macadamia nuts, pine nuts, natural peanut butter (crunchy), almond butter, sesame butter (tahini), sunflower seeds, pistachios, Brazil nuts

  HELPFUL HINTS: Be sure to read the "Omegasizing" Your Meals (page 35) to learn how to grind and toast flaxseeds as well as some interesting ways to use them in your recipes.

- **Protein foods:** Eggs (preferably omega-3 enriched such as Gold Circle Farms, the Country Hen, Egg-land's Best, Born "3" and Pilgrim's Pride Eggs Plus), tofu (firm and silken), tempeh

  HELPFUL HINTS: The egg manufacturers mentioned above feed hens omega-3–enriched foods to obtain a nutritionally fortified egg that provides more unsaturated fat. When it comes to eggs, fresh is always best. So use yours within one week of purchase. Also, be sure to change the water in opened tofu daily.

- **Dairy products:** Sweet butter, cheeses (low-fat ricotta cheese, low-fat cottage cheese, part-skim mozzarella or string cheese, feta, goat cheese, cheddar, Parmesan, Swiss), low-fat plain yogurt, sour cream, buttermilk

- **Vegetables:** Artichokes, asparagus, broccoli, brussels sprouts, cabbage, carrots, cauliflower, celery, cucumbers, daikon radishes, radishes, chilis, leafy greens, kale, endive, romaine lettuce, red leaf lettuce, arugula, lemon grass, leeks, mushrooms, alfalfa sprouts, sweet potatoes, squash (butternut, spaghetti, summer, zucchini), Swiss chard, tomatoes (roma, plum, cherry), turnips, watercress, yams, parsnips, beets, green beans, sun-dried tomatoes, tomatillos, onions, shallots, chives, scallions, jicama, spinach, peppers (orange, yellow, red, green), string beans

- **Fruits:** Apples, avocados, berries (seasonal), oranges, grapefruit, kiwi fruit, pears, plums, peaches, pineapple, nectarines, honeydew, cantaloupe, cherries, papaya, mango, limes, lemons, umeboshi plums, tangerines

- **Cooking liquids:** Filtered water, Pacific almond milk, rice milk, papaya juice concentrate, low-sodium broths (chicken, beef, vegetable), clamato juice, unsweetened cranberry, apple, and orange juice

- **Condiments:** Fresh basil and parsley, fresh cilantro, fresh garlic, Spectrum Naturals organic mayonnaise, Dijon mustard, honey mustard, tamari, Tabasco or hot sauce, low-sodium soy sauce, jerk seasoning, Worcestershire sauce, ginger, sauerkraut, horseradish, Thai Kitchen Fish Sauce, Westbrae Natural Fruit Sweetened Catsup, salsa, marinara sauce, tomato sauce, tomato purée, Classico Roasted Garlic Sauce, unsweetened applesauce

The *Eat Fat, Lose Weight* Freezer

- **Protein foods:** Beef flank steak, stew beef, lean ground chuck, ground sirloin, chicken breasts, fish fillets, scallops, salmon fillets, tuna steaks, shelled and deveined shrimp, veal cutlets and ground veal, leg of lamb, ground lamb, Shelton's Turkey Sausage, ground turkey, sea bass, orange roughy, red snapper, lox, pork chops, pork medallions
- **Vegetables:** Asparagus, chopped spinach, peas, broccoli, okra, green beans, succotash
- **Fruits:** Unsweetened blueberries, raspberries, blackberries, strawberries
- **Flour:** Forti-Flax Flour, Bob's Red Mill Flaxseed Meal, whole grain flour, spelt flour, soy flour, cornmeal

   HELPFUL HINTS: All flours do best in the freezer or fridge to keep them fresh and free from weevils and other uninvited guests.

The *Eat Fat, Lose Weight* Pantry

- **Oils:** Extra-virgin, virgin, or unfiltered olive, sesame, toasted sesame, high-oleic safflower, high-oleic sunflower

   HELPFUL HINTS: Extra-virgin, virgin, and unfiltered virgin olive oils are rich and full bodied because they are derived from the first pressing. The fruity flavors of the virgin olive oils lend themselves beautifully to salads. Unfiltered olive oil that contains olive bits is a real treat over veggies.

- **Canned fish:** Tuna (Progresso Light Tuna in Olive Oil, Chicken of the Sea White Tuna in Spring Water), salmon, oysters, anchovies, sardines

- **Condiments:** Nonirradiated dried herbs and spices, such as dill, tarragon, basil, garlic, marjoram, coriander, fennel seeds, anise seed, bay leaf, cloves, cardamom, ginger, cinnamon, nutmeg, thyme, dry mustard, rosemary, cumin, oregano, cayenne, chili powder, savory, mint or peppermint, crushed pepper flakes, paprika, allspice, peppercorns, sea salt, saffron threads, red curry paste, low-sodium tamari, vinegar (apple cider, balsamic, red wine, raspberry, rice), all-fruit jams, stevia, artichoke hearts, green olives with pimientos, kalamata olives, black olives, capers, sun-dried tomatoes, hearts of palm, bamboo shoots, water chestnuts, baby corn

- **Special occasion recipe liquids:** Thai Kitchen Lite Pure Coconut Milk, Ceres mango, papaya, and apricot juices, wines (such as Marsala or dry white wine)

  HELPFUL HINTS: 1 tablespoon of coconut milk equals 1 teaspoon of oil; 2 tablespoons of shredded coconut equals 1 tablespoon of fat.

- **Fruits:** Bananas and dried, unsulfured apricots, raisins, cranberries, prunes, figs

- **Starches:** Corn tortillas, whole grain breads, bagels, English muffins, pita bread, rye bread or crackers, Sun Luck Bean Threads (mung bean noodles), barley, brown rice, basmati rice, popcorn, wheat germ, fresh or canned corn, potatoes, bread crumbs

- **Beans:** Black beans, kidney beans, navy beans, chickpeas or garbanzo beans, lentils, split peas, cannellini beans

- **Baking needs:** Aluminum-free baking powder (Rumford, Royal, or Featherweight brands), arrowroot, steel-cut oats, stone-ground cornmeal, whole wheat or white pastry flour, spelt flour, soy flour, blackstrap molasses, 100 percent maple syrup, rice syrup, honey, carob powder, granulated tapioca, coconut flakes, Bickford or Frontier nonalcohol vanilla, anise, almond, and lemon extracts

- **Miscellaneous:** Protein powders (Solgar's Whey to Go, Naturade's Fat-Free Vegetable Protein), Designer Protein Whey, low-sodium V-8 juice

CHAPTER THREE

THE MASTER DIET BLUEPRINT

ow you're ready for the easy, ten-step diet blueprint. It's the plan we used to create the delicious *Eat Fat, Lose Weight* menus and recipes, ensuring the program was optimally healthy every step of the way. It may sound a little academic at first, but give it a chance. Remember, it's just a blueprint. Our entire goal is to help you gain *portion savvy* and *omega know-how*. That way you'll have a good foundation for understanding how to balance your diet with deliciously filling meals every day of the week and lose weight at the same time. In fact, there's one food group (the starch family) where you will learn to add or subtract, depending on your individual weight-loss needs.

1. *Fish: 3 to 4 ounces of omega-3 fatty fish two to three times per week.**
   The best choices include salmon, rainbow trout, herring, sardines, mackerel, and tuna.

   *Those who aren't fish lovers should supplement their diets with 1,000 mg Super MaxEPA two to three times daily to meet the omega-3 requirements.

2. *Omega-3–rich foods: at least one serving daily.*
   Each of the following omega-3 food sources contains the equivalent of 1 tablespoon of oil. Choose one of the following each day:
   - 1 tablespoon flaxseed oil
   - 3 tablespoons ground flaxseeds
   - 1 tablespoon walnut oil
   - 1 tablespoon Essential Woman Oil
   - 1 tablespoon Spectrum Naturals organic mayonnaise
   - 1 tablespoon pumpkin seeds

- 2 medium Brazil nuts
- 4 walnut halves or 1 tablespoon chopped walnuts
- 3 fillet anchovies (well rinsed)

3. *Omega-9–rich foods: at least one serving daily.*
   Each of the following omega-9 sources contains the equivalent of 1 tablespoon of oil. Choose one of the following each day:
   - 1 tablespoon extra-virgin or virgin olive oil
   - 1 tablespoon peanut oil
   - 1 tablespoon high-oleic sunflower oil*
   - 1 tablespoon high-oleic safflower oil*
   - ⅛ medium avocado
   - 8 large black olives
   - 1 tablespoon nut butter (peanut, almond, sesame, tahini)
   - Shelled nuts:
       7 almonds
       5 cashews
       10 peanuts
       4 pecan halves
       3 macadamia nuts
   - Seeds: 1 tablespoon sesame seeds

   High-oleic sunflower and safflower oils (omega-9 oils) tolerate high heat well, making them great for frying and stir-frying.

4. *Omega-6–rich foods: at least one serving twice a week.*
   Each of the following omega-6 sources contains the equivalent of 1 tablespoon of oil.
   - Shelled nuts:
       1 tablespoon pine nuts
       15 pistachios
   - Seeds: 1 tablespoon sunflower seeds
   - Cereals: 3 tablespoons wheat germ

   Those who would rather take an omega-6 supplement than eat these nuts and seeds can substitute 500 mg (one capsule per meal) of borage oil, or 500 mg (two to four capsules per meal) of evening primrose oil, or two capsules per meal of black currant seed oil (GLA-90) daily. Those who have a lot of weight to lose might add 1,000 mg of conjugated linoleic acid (CLA) before each meal.

5. *Protein: at least 6 to 8 ounces of protein daily.*

   Be sure to have a serving of protein at breakfast, lunch, and dinner. Choose organic foods when possible to avoid hormones and other chemical additives.

   Protein Serving Sizes:
   - 2 eggs
   - 3 ounces cooked meat (veal, poultry, beef, pork, lamb)
   - 6 ounces fish or shellfish
   - ½ cup tofu or tempeh

6. *Fruit: at least two servings daily.*

   Fruits are loaded with enzymes, minerals (such as potassium), vitamin C, and fiber, which are potent disease fighters and natural cleansers for the system.

   In general, one serving equals ½ cup chopped fruit or one medium piece of fruit. These fruits are recommended as healthy between-meal snacks. For those of you concerned about your carbohydrate intake, each fruit serving listed below is about 15 carbohydrate grams.

   Fresh Fruits:
   - 2 plums
   - 1 apple, pear, nectarine, peach, or kiwi fruit
   - 1 cup cantaloupe or honeydew cubes
   - ¾ cup blueberries
   - 1 cup raspberries
   - 1¼ cups strawberries
   - ½ grapefruit
   - ½ cup unsweetened applesauce
   - ½ papaya, mango, or banana
   - ½ cup unsweetened pineapple
   - 10 grapes
   - 12 cherries

   Dried Fruits:
   - 2 medium prunes
   - 2 dates
   - 8 dried apricot halves
   - 2 tablespoons raisins or dried cranberries

Juices:

- ½ cup orange juice
- ½ cup grapefruit juice
- ⅓ cup apple juice

Fruit Preserves and Jams:

- 2 tablespoons apple butter
- 2 tablespoons unsweetened fruit preserves of any kind

7. *Vegetables: at least five servings daily from a rainbow of colorful veggies.* Vegetables are an outstanding source of antioxidants and phytochemicals (plant-based healing substances). The lycopene in tomatoes, the lutein in kale, and the flavonoids in rich, colorful red-orange veggies protect against disease and help slow down the aging process.

One serving equals ½ cup cooked vegetables, 1 cup leafy greens, 1 cup raw vegetables, or ¾ cup vegetable juice, unless otherwise noted. Choose organic whenever possible to avoid pesticides, herbicides, and fungicides. Each serving is equal to 5 carbohydrate grams except for raw onions, tomatoes, and beets, which are 10 carbohydrates each.

Cooked (½ cup each):

- broccoli
- daikon radish
- okra
- cauliflower
- summer squash
- zucchini
- collard greens
- eggplant
- spaghetti squash
- beans, green or yellow
- snow peas
- mushrooms
- cabbage
- brussels sprouts
- sauerkraut
- red or green peppers
- Chinese cabbage

Leafy Greens:

- escarole
- kale
- chard
- dandelion
- mustard
- spinach
- radicchio
- arugula
- broccoli rabe
- romaine lettuce
- red or green leaf lettuce
- watercress

Raw Vegetables:

- 1 onion (2½ inches)
- 1 tomato (2½ inches)
- 1 medium beet (2 inches)
- ½ cup jicama
- 4 water chestnuts
- 1 cup broccoli
- 1 cup cauliflower
- 1 cup cucumbers
- 1 large carrot
- 1 cup radishes
- 1 cup sprouts: mung bean, adzuki, alfalfa, clover, radish
- 1 cup endive
- 1 cup celery

8. *Carbohydrates: at least two servings daily from high-fiber carbohydrates such as whole grain breads, cereals, pastas, beans, and starchy vegetables.* Dietary fiber is important for keeping your bowels regular. Carbohydrate intake can be flexible. Once your weight-loss goals are reached, you may add more carbohydrates, one serving at a time— for example, an extra slice of whole grain toast at breakfast or a small sweet potato at dinner.

One serving equals one slice of whole grain bread, ½ cup of brown rice, or ½ cup of starchy vegetables or beans. Breakfast is the best time to eat your carbohydrate servings since you have the rest of the day to burn them off. Please note that each serving is equal to 15 carbohydrate grams.

Breads/Crackers:

- 4 whole wheat crackers
- 4 rice crackers
- 4 rice cakes
- 2 crisp rye breads or wafers
- 1 slice whole grain bread
- 1 corn tortilla
- ½ whole grain pita pocket
- ½ whole grain English muffin
- ½ slice pumpernickel bread
- ½ whole grain bagel
- ½ whole wheat matzo

Cereals and Grains:

- 1 ounce or 3 tablespoons wheat germ
- 5 cups air-popped popcorn
- ⅓ cup cooked barley
- ⅓ cup cooked brown or basmati rice

Flours:

- 2 tablespoons arrowroot flour
- 3 tablespoons whole wheat flour
- 3 tablespoons spelt flour
- ½ cup almond meal
- ½ cup soy flour
- ½ cup flax flour or flaxmeal

Pasta:

- ½ cup whole wheat, spelt, or rice noodles
- ¾ cup mung bean noodles

Beans:

- ½ cup navy, lima, kidney, black, pinto, garbanzo, or soy beans
- ½ cup lentils or split peas
- ⅓ cup lima beans

Starchy Cooked Vegetables:
- ½ cup winter squash
- ¾ cup peas
- ½ cup corn
- ½ cup butternut or acorn squash
- 1 small baked potato with skin
- ½ cup succotash
- ¾ cup pumpkin
- 1 small sweet potato
- 1 parsnip
- 1 small rutabaga
- 4 large or 6 small chestnuts

9. *Dairy: at least one to two low-fat dairy servings daily.*

   One serving equals ¾ cup nonfat or low-fat plain yogurt, 1 ounce low-fat cheese, or ½ cup skim or low-fat ricotta or cottage cheese. It is best to choose organic dairy foods whenever possible.

   CARB WATCHERS: Each 6 ounces (¾ cup) nonfat or low-fat yogurt is equal to 12 carbohydrate grams.
   - 6 ounces plain nonfat or low-fat yogurt
   - 4 ounces skim ricotta or low-fat cottage cheese
   - 1 ounce Swiss or cheddar cheese
   - 1½ ounces part-skim mozzarella cheese
   - 8 ounces nonfat cow's or goat's milk
   - 1 ounces farmer's or goat's cheese
   - 1 ounce Sago cheese
   - 1 ounce string cheese

10. *Water and other liquids: at least eight glasses of water daily, preferably between meals.*

    Choose herbal teas and naturally decaffeinated coffees instead of regular tea and coffee.

CHAPTER FOUR

TWENTY-ONE-DAY MENU PLAN

N ow that you have the foundation for our *Eat Fat, Lose Weight* diet plan, it's time to put it all together into a sample three-week eating program. First, let's recap the main points of our master blueprint.

1. *"Omegasize" your diet.* Eat fatty fish at least two to three times a week. Include servings of omega-3– and omega-9–rich foods each day and an omega-6 food, snack, or supplement at least twice a week.
2. *Power up on protein.* Include 6 to 8 ounces of protein daily.
3. *Sweeten up with fruits.* Enjoy at least two fruit servings daily—a perfect choice for morning smoothies or snacks.
4. *Vibrate with veggies.* Choose at least five colorful vegetables daily.
5. *Satisfy with starches.* Enjoy at least one to two servings of grain; colorful, starchy vegetable; and/or beans daily.
6. *Dare with dairy.* Include at least one to two servings of low-fat dairy servings daily.
7. *H_2O to the rescue.* Drink at least eight glasses of pure water each day.

We've designed the *Eat Fat, Lose Weight* menu plan for *real* people, those who are busy practically every day of the week and who may or may not have the desire to cook fancy meals. So we've kept breakfast easy with simple-to-make smoothies and quick egg dishes. For lunch, we've suggested many main-course salad recipes for fast noontime meals. If you eat out for lunch on workdays, don't fret. Just check the recipe ingredients in the following luncheon menus, and choose something fairly similar at a restaurant. You'll find chicken or seafood salads on most menus across the country. And if you're unsure of what dressing to order, simply squeeze a lemon on your salad for a tasty (yet healthy) alternative.

While looking over the Twenty-One-Day Menu Plan and recipe section, remember:

- The *Eat Fat, Lose Weight Cookbook* recipes appearing on the Twenty-One-Day Menu Plan include the page numbers where you can find them.

- Many recipes are one-meal dishes, containing a number of the *Eat Fat, Lose Weight* food groups. For example, one of our favorite recipes, Hawaiian Chicken Salad, is made with pineapple and macadamia nuts, so it's rich in protein, vegetables, fruits, and omega oils. (The pineapple in this recipe counts as one of the allowed fruit servings for the day, which means you'll have to adjust the rest of your day's fruit intake accordingly.)

- Meat, poultry, and fish portions should always measure at least 3 ounces.

- We have indicated in the Twenty-One-Day Menu Plan which recipes and foods are an omega source. When you create your own menu plans, however, resist the temptation to overdo it by having every item in your meal comprise these healthy fats. One to two items will do.

- High-carbohydrate recipes are noted with an asterisk (*) in the recipe section.

- Feel free to diversify the menu plan to suit your individual taste by referring back to the Master Diet Blueprint. Simply exchange one food for another from the same food category.

Week 1

Monday

Breakfast:

1 scrambled egg with spinach and mushrooms sautéed in
1 tablespoon extra-virgin olive oil (omega-9)
1 slice whole grain bread

Midmorning Snack:

1 apple

Lunch:

Hawaiian Chicken Salad (page 92; omega-3 and omega-9)

Midafternoon Snack:

1 ounce string cheese

Dinner:

Mama's Meatloaf (page 138)
Steamed string beans
Mixed green salad with cucumbers, tomatoes, and sprouts drizzled
with Templeton's Best Dressing (page 99; omega-3 and omega-9)

Tuesday

Breakfast:

6 ounces orange juice
Cheesy muffin topped with tomato (sprinkle 1 or 2 ounces shredded,
part-skim mozzarella cheese over ½ whole grain English muffin,
broiling until cheese melts)

Midmorning Snack:

15 pistachios (omega-6)

Lunch:

Sunny Caesar Salad (page 90; omega-3 and omega-9)

Midafternoon Snack:

1 pear
1 tablespoon pumpkin seeds (omega-3)

Dinner:

Grilled chicken breast with tarragon and parsley
Steamed asparagus

Chopped parsley, tomatoes, and scallions drizzled with
2 teaspoons apple cider vinegar, 1 tablespoon olive oil (omega-9),
and dash of mint

Wednesday

Breakfast:

4 dried apricot halves and 4 walnut halves (omega-3) chopped into
1 cup plain yogurt

Midmorning Snack:

1 ounce sliced cheddar cheese

1 corn tortilla

Lunch:

California Salmon Salad (page 94; omega-3 and omega-9)

Midafternoon Snack:

4 pecan halves (omega-9)

Dinner:

Saucy Red Cabbage (page 106; omega-9)

Skinned turkey breast with fennel

Steamed broccoli with lemon juice

1 small sweet potato

Thursday

Breakfast:

Berry-Nut Smoothie (page 45; omega-3 and omega-9)

Midmorning Snack:

1 tablespoon peanut butter on celery sticks (omega-9)

Lunch:

Tofu and vegetable stir-fry (6 ounces tofu sautéed with water chestnuts, bok choy, baby corn, and bamboo shoots in 1 tablespoon
peanut oil) (omega-9)

½ cup brown rice or rice noodles

Midafternoon Snack:

1 cup cantaloupe

Dinner:

Grilled salmon (omega-3)

Sautéed mushrooms in white wine
½ cup green peas
Spinach and pimiento salad drizzled with balsamic vinegar

Friday

Breakfast:
½ cup low-fat cottage cheese with
1 tablespoon Essential Woman Oil (omega-3 and omega-6)
½ cup pineapple chunks
1 slice rye toast

Midmorning Snack:
1¼ cups strawberries

Lunch:
Lean beef burger smothered with sautéed onions
Romaine lettuce, grated jicama, and tomato salad drizzled with
1 tablespoon each extra-virgin olive oil (omega-9) and
    apple cider vinegar

Midafternoon Snack:
1 ounce sliced Swiss cheese

Dinner:
Tuna and Salsa Supreme (page 132; omega-3 and omega-9)
Steamed cauliflower drizzled with
1 tablespoon walnut oil (omega-3)
Kale sautéed with tomatoes

Saturday

Breakfast:
Heavenly Pancakes (page 51; omega-3) topped with
¾ cup blueberries or 1¼ cups strawberries (omega-3)

Midmorning Snack:
1 tablespoon sunflower seeds (omega-6)

Lunch:
Arugula, chicory, and endive salad drizzled with
1 tablespoon each extra-virgin olive oil (omega-9) and lemon juice
Green Goddess Frittata (page 58)

Midafternoon Snack:

1 pear

Dinner:

Celery, cucumber spears, and radishes with
½ cup Avocado-Cilantro Dip (page 59; omega-3 and omega-9)
Flavorful Flank Steak (page 136; omega-9)
½ cup butternut squash

Sunday

Breakfast:

1 cup low-sodium V-8 juice
One-Two-Three Huevos Rancheros (page 54; omega-9)
1 warm corn tortilla
1 ounce low-fat mozzarella cheese

Midmorning Snack:

1 orange

Lunch:

Outrageous Tuna Burgers (page 133; omega-3 and omega-9)
Steamed string beans with water chestnuts
Sicilian Bliss (page 108; omega-9)

Midafternoon Snack:

1 cup low-fat plain yogurt blended with
¼ teaspoon vanilla extract and ½ teaspoon cinnamon

Dinner:

Crunchy Chicken (page 143; omega-9)
Jicama Slaw (page 107; omega-3)
Sautéed collard greens and fennel in chicken broth

Week 2

Monday

Breakfast:

Arctic Smoothie (page 47; omega-3 and omega-6)

Midmorning Snack:

15 pistachios (omega-6)

Lunch:

South Sea Crab Salad (page 97; omega-3 and omega-9) drizzled with Citrus-Twister Dressing (page 103; omega-3)

Midafternoon Snack:

1 ounce string cheese on 2 crisp rye crackers

Dinner:

Monday-Night Chicken Stir-Fry (page 144; omega-9)

⅓ cup basmati rice

Tuesday

Breakfast:

½ cup banana blended in

1 cup low-fat plain yogurt topped with

2 medium Brazil nuts (omega-3), chopped

Midmorning Snack:

1 tablespoon sunflower seeds (omega 6)

Lunch:

Lean broiled turkey burger with ⅛ teaspoon fennel

Steamed green beans

Chopped parsley, onion, and tomato salad drizzled with

French Riviera Dressing (page 100; omega-9)

Midafternoon Snack:

2 rye crackers

1 ounce Swiss cheese

Dinner:

Veal strips cooked in white wine and garlic

Zucchini and tomato sauté

⅓ cup brown rice

Salad greens with

Pepita Plum Dressing (page 100; omega-3)

Wednesday

Breakfast:

½ cup fresh fruit salad blended in

½ cup low-fat cottage cheese topped with

7 almonds (omega-9), chopped

Midmorning Snack:

    Celery sticks with 1 tablespoon peanut butter (omega-9)

Lunch:

    Red snapper topped with

    That's Italian Pesto (page 64; omega-3 and omega-9)

    Steamed asparagus with lemon

    ½ baked acorn squash sprinkled with nutmeg

Midafternoon Snack:

    1 tangerine

    1 ounce cheddar cheese

Dinner:

    Southwest Salisbury Steak (page 137; omega-3 and omega-9)

    1 small baked potato drizzled with ½ teaspoon flaxseed oil (omega-3)

    Mixed green salad drizzled with apple cider vinegar

Thursday

Breakfast:

    Luscious Melon Smoothie (page 45; omega-3 and omega-9)

Midmorning Snack:

    1 tablespoon roasted pine nuts (omega-6)

Lunch:

    Poached orange roughy with lemon and capers

    Steamed green beans

    1 small corn on the cob

    Sliced tomato and parsley salad drizzled with

    1 tablespoon each peanut oil (omega-9), lemon juice, and

        apple cider vinegar

Midafternoon Snack:

    1 nectarine

    1 ounce Swiss cheese

Dinner:

    Grilled tenderloin steak with garlic and mushrooms

    ½ cup green peas with pearl onions

    ½ cup butternut squash

    Wilted greens drizzled with

    Balsamic-Hazelnut Dressing (page 101; omega-9)

Friday

Breakfast:

1¼ cups strawberries (omega-3)

1 cup plain low-fat yogurt blended with

1 tablespoon Essential Woman Oil (omega-3 and omega-6)

Midmorning Snack:

1 pear

1 tablespoon pumpkin seeds (omega-3)

Lunch:

1 cup Mushroom Barley Soup (page 78; omega-3 and omega-9)

Lean hamburger patty topped with tomato slices, bermuda onion, and pickles

Leafy green salad drizzled with

1 tablespoon each extra-virgin olive oil (omega-9) and balsamic vinegar

Midafternoon Snack:

1 ounce cheddar cheese

Dinner:

Eggplant Tapenade (page 62; omega-9) with veggie sticks

Grilled lamb chop with cumin and cinnamon

Steamed okra

Warm cauliflower tossed with apple cider vinegar

Saturday

Breakfast:

Some-Like-It-Hot Poached Eggs (page 55; omega-3 and omega-6) made with Healthy Fun Twist (omega-3)

½ cup unsweetened applesauce

Midmorning Snack:

Celery sticks topped with

1 ounce goat cheese

Lunch:

Mango Salmon Salad (page 95; omega-3 and omega-9)

Midafternoon Snack:

2 rye crackers and 1 tablespoon almond butter (omega-9)

Dinner:

Asian Stir-Fry (page 135; omega-3 and omega-9)

⅓ cup brown rice

Sunday

Breakfast:

2 Blueberry Yogurt Flaxjacks (page 52; omega-3 and omega-9)

Midmorning Snack:

2 plums

Lunch:

Olive-Tuna Salad (page 95; omega-3 and omega-9)

1 cup vegetable broth

Midafternoon Snack:

1 ounce cheddar cheese

1 Granny Smith apple

Dinner:

Grilled lamb chops with rosemary

1 cup stir-fried vegetables over

¾ cup mung bean noodles topped with

1 tablespoon sesame seeds (omega-9)

Week 3

Monday

Breakfast:

½ grapefruit

2 eggs scrambled in 1 tablespoon extra-virgin olive oil (omega-9) with
3 ounces part-skim mozzarella cheese, scallions, and tomatoes

Midmorning Snack:

¾ cup mixed berries

Lunch:

Tex-Mex Salad (page 91; omega-3 and omega-9) drizzled with
Lime-Cilantro Vinaigrette (page 99; omega-3)

Midafternoon Snack:

2 small carrot sticks with 1 tablespoon almond butter (omega-9)

Dinner:

Grilled salmon fillets (omega-3) topped with
Tangy Tapenade (page 62; omega-3 and omega-9)
Sliced tomato, radish, and cucumber salad
Steamed pea pods and red bell peppers

Tuesday

Breakfast:

1 cup raspberries blended into
½ cup low-fat cottage cheese topped with
3 tablespoons toasted wheat germ (omega-6)

Midmorning Snack:

Cucumber spears with
1 tablespoon tahini (omega-9)

Lunch:

Basil-Garlic Seafood Salad (page 98; omega-3)

Midafternoon Snack:

1 nectarine with 1 ounce string cheese

Dinner:

Veal Stew (page 89; omega-9)
Spaghetti Squash Toss (page 114; omega-9)
½ cup succotash

Wednesday

Breakfast:

Pineapple-Pecan Smoothie (page 46; omega-3 and omega-9)

Midmorning Snack:

1 tablespoon sunflower seeds (omega-6)
1 ounce sliced Swiss cheese

Lunch:

Sardines (omega-3) with chopped tomatoes, parsley, and scallions
drizzled with
Pepita Plum Dressing (page 100; omega-3)

Midafternoon Snack:

1 Granny Smith apple

Dinner:
Pork medallions topped with Paradise Salsa (page 68; omega-3)
½ cup butternut squash spiced with cinnamon
Watercress and hearts of palm drizzled with raspberry vinegar

Thursday

Breakfast:
Peanut Butter Crunch Smoothie (page 44; omega-9)

Midmorning Snack:
1 peach

Lunch:
Broiled lamb or beef patty with rosemary and mint
Ratatouille
1 small sweet potato

Midafternoon Snack:
4 walnut halves (omega-3) with
1 tablespoon raisins

Dinner:
Sliced turkey breast cooked with fennel and topped with
Tomato-Basil Salsa (page 67; omega-3 and omega-9)
Roasted red pepper, olive, and broccoli toss
⅓ cup steamed basmati or brown rice

Friday

Breakfast:
Pacific Coast Smoothie (page 46; omega-3 and omega-9)

Midmorning Snack:
1 pear

Lunch:
2 boiled eggs
2 rye crackers or 1 slice multigrain bread
Cucumber, tomato, and hearts of palm salad drizzled with
Balsamic vinegar and 1 tablespoon olive oil (omega-9)

Midafternoon Snack:
1 nectarine

Dinner:

1 cup vegetable broth

Snapper Crunch (page 120; omega-3 and omega-9)

Steamed bok choy, spinach, broccoli, and carrots

¾ cup mung bean noodles

Saturday

Breakfast:

½ cup orange juice

Rainbow Veggie Omelet (page 56)

1 slice Flax-for-Thought Bread (page 48; omega-3)

Midmorning Snack:

1 pear with

1 tablespoon tahini (omega-9)

Lunch:

Diced chicken blended with

1 tablespoon Spectrum Naturals organic mayonnaise (omega-3) and
celery over a bed of field greens drizzled with apple cider vinegar

Midafternoon Snack:

½ cup Middle Eastern Hummus (page 60; omega-3 and omega-9)
with daikon radish and green and red pepper strips

Dinner:

Lamb or Veal Kebobs (page 150; omega-3 and omega-9)

Steamed artichoke with

1 tablespoon garlic-infused extra-virgin olive oil (omega-9)

Minty Mashed Cauliflower (page 117)

Sunday

Breakfast:

½ grapefruit

Zesty-Quick Scramblers (page 53; omega-9)

3 ounces lox (omega-3)

1 slice whole grain bread, toasted

Midmorning Snack:
  2 Spinach-Walnut-Stuffed Mushrooms (page 70; omega-3 and omega-9)

Lunch:
  1 cup Cucumber Dill Soup (page 84: omega-3 and omega-9)
  Baked pork chop topped with
  ¼ cup Basil-Flax Aioli (page 63; omega-3)
  Wilted collard greens, kale, and mustard greens

Midafternoon Snack:
  1 nectarine
  1 ounce string cheese

Dinner:
  Cuban-Style Turkey Breast (page 147) topped with
  ½ cup Black Bean and Peanut Salsa (page 68; omega-9)
  Okra and zucchini sauté
  Cubed avocado salad (omega-9) spiked with lemon juice

CHAPTER FIVE

"OMEGASIZING" YOUR MEALS

on't worry. Powering up your meals with the health-promoting omega oils is really a snap. You can easily slip healthy fats into breakfast, lunch, dinner, or snacks—without family members even realizing it! Here are a few easy tips to get you started.

1. *Use omega-3–enriched eggs.* Many health food stores and natural supermarkets stock them.

2. *Use less sugar.* This is the way to avoid empty calories, high insulin levels, and subsequently, fat storage.

3. *Cook with monounsaturated oils only.* Use extra-virgin olive oil or peanut oil, both high in omega-9.

4. *Tap into the power of flax.* Hands down, one of the most effective ways to promote better health, feel good, and look even better is by adding omega-3–rich flax to your meals—flaxseeds, flaxmeal, or flaxseed oil. That's why you'll find it in many of our recipes. In fact, I'm such a firm believer in the power of flax and botanicals that I helped formulate a product called Essential Woman Oil. This delicate blend of flax oil, evening primrose oil, and isoflavones can be used in recipes or taken daily. You can spread it on toast in the morning, mix it in yogurt or cottage cheese, or even drizzle it on steamed veggies and air-popped popcorn. Essential Woman Oil is available at many health food stores nationwide or through Uni Key Health Systems (see Resources).

Hop on the Flax Track

The benefits of flaxseed are nothing short of extraordinary. Besides having an extremely high omega-3 content, flaxseed is also rich in dietary fiber and lignans. The soluble fiber aids in reducing carbohydrate absorption, stabilizing blood sugar levels, inhibiting cholesterol absorption, and lowering blood cholesterol levels. The insoluble fiber absorbs water in the digestive tract to ease elimination, making it a great help with bowel problems such as constipation and diverticular disease. Lignans—which are concentrated 800 times more in whole flaxseed than in other plants—are recognized for their cancer-fighting benefits, antiviral properties, and helping to alleviate perimenopause and menopause symptoms. Also, a mounting number of scientific studies show the omega-3 power found in flaxseed to improve heart disease, arthritis, multiple sclerosis, breast cancer, lupus, liver disorders; to heal bruises and sprains, mental function and depression, eczema, psoriasis, acne, and dry skin—and this isn't even a complete list of its health benefits. In addition, athletes praise its ability to help maintain energy levels and increase stamina.

Kids and Flax

Perhaps the most remarkable news about omega-3–rich flax is its dramatic effect on children. Paul Stitt, a baker in Wisconsin, put flaxseed oil in his baked goods and gave them to an elementary school. Both parents and teachers reported a noticeable improvement in students' behavior. This is no coincidence. It all stems from the omega-3s having a tremendous impact on brain function. Anytime there are changes to the brain cell membranes, you're bound to see a switch in behavior.

With that as their basis, researchers conducted numerous studies over the past two decades demonstrating that kids with ADHD (attention deficit hyperactivity disorder) had lower omega-3 and/or omega-6 levels in their blood than their normal counterparts. Study after study also revealed that these same fatty acid–deficient kids were more prone to learning, behavioral, and even health problems. Even more startling research demonstrated that treating these children with medication, psychology, and special education was not enough. They were still liable to participate in harmful behavior such as drug abuse and petty crimes.

Clearly, the missing link in this lopsided equation is responsible nutrition that features omega oils. Without a doubt, bumping up every meal with omega-enriched foods and recipes is a wise choice for parents everywhere.

Flax-Track Tips

- Use flaxseed whole or grind to the consistency of finely ground coffee. Just pour whole flaxseeds into a coffee grinder, blender, or food processor, choosing the fine setting. Although ground flaxseed can be stored for a short time in the refrigerator, you will get the most nutritional benefit by grinding the seeds as needed.

- An easier option is Forti-Flax, available in health food stores. This coarse-ground product has the consistency of flour and is ready for use, especially in our omega-rich muffins and pancakes. Thanks to its partially defatted quality, Forti-Flax won't clump up like full-fat flax flour.

- Store whole flaxseed at room temperature up to a year. Store ground flaxseed in your refrigerator for up to ninety days.

- When you're using whole flaxseeds in baked goods, soak them for 10 minutes before adding them to the batter.

Other Easy Ways to Add Flax to Your Diet

- Flax spread is a flavorful butter that everyone will love. Smear it on muffins, breads, pancakes, or anything else on which you'd use butter.

    Simply cube one stick of butter and toss it in a saucepan over low heat until it lightly melts. Then pour the melted butter into a small storage container. Add 4 ounces of flax oil and stir until blended. Cover the mixture with the container lid and store in the refrigerator until it solidifies.

- Delicious and nutritiously healthy, flaxseed tea helps cleanse toxins from the kidneys and combat intestinal irritations (such as colitis) or mucous membrane inflammations.

    Steep 1 teaspoon of flaxseeds in 10 ounces of boiling water for 20 minutes. Strain and enjoy with your breakfast, lunch, or dinner.

- Blend 1 part flax oil with 1 part maple syrup for a flavorful topping over pancakes—perfect for kids.

- Toast flaxmeal and blend it with honey for a topping on cereal, cottage cheese, yogurt, or fruit, much as you would use toasted wheat germ.

- Flaxmeal (and even nuts) can be home-toasted in the oven at 250°F. Heating above 300°F damages the oil and changes it into the unhealthy trans form. Spread flaxmeal on a baking sheet, place in the oven at 225° to 250°F, and bake until crispy (about 15 to 20 minutes).
- Mix flax oil into hot cereal for a rich, nutty taste. (It's also a good bowel regulator, especially helpful for kids.)
- Blend 1 tablespoon of flax oil into yogurt and stir in some fruit.
- Drizzle flax oil over veggies and season to taste.

Flax and Baking

- Use flax in place of fat. Substitute 3 tablespoons ground flaxseed for 1 tablespoon cooking oil, butter, or margarine. Note: Your baked goods will brown more quickly with flax, so either shorten baking time or lower oven temperature by 25°.
- Use flax instead of eggs. Blend 1 tablespoon ground flax with 3 tablespoons water and let stand for a couple of minutes, then use in place of one egg for muffins, breads, or pancakes. If you're allergic or sensitive to eggs, this is a great alternative.
- Use flaxmeal in place of some flour. You can purchase flaxmeal at grocery stores and health food markets, or grind flaxseeds and make your own. Just be sure to grind them to a wheat germ–like consistency. Here's how: Take 2 tablespoons out of each cup of flour, and replace it with 2 tablespoons of flaxmeal. While you're at it, you can also reduce the oil in the recipe, since flax is loaded with healthy fats. As a rule of thumb, omit 1 tablespoon of oil for every 3 tablespoons of flaxmeal added. (Remember, as noted above, baked goods will brown more quickly using flax. Bake for a shorter time or lower heat by 25°.) For best results if you're using flax in a yeast recipe, increase the amount of yeast by 25 percent and slightly increase the water.

   Added tip: Since flaxmeal doesn't contain gluten (needed for bread to rise), consider adding 1 tablespoon of gluten for every ½ cup flaxmeal you use (provided you're not gluten sensitive).

CHAPTER SIX

THE FAT ZAPPERS

I n addition to the *Eat Fat, Lose Weight* dietary program, my personal nutrition clients have used the following nutritional supplements and fat burners with outstanding success. I have helped to develop many of these formulas. They are available through Uni Key Health Systems (see Resources).

Conjugated linoleic acid (CLA) certainly tops the list. Over a hundred remarkable new studies reveal CLA as an incredible fat burner. A Norwegian study demonstrated that CLA actually revs up your fat-burning potential and helps reduce body fat by up to 20 percent. It does this by controlling the enzymatic action that emits fat into the bloodstream, according to research conducted at the University of Wisconsin. CLA also permeates muscle cells, where it increases muscle mass by 5 percent. In fact, research revealed that just by taking a daily dose of CLA, women could potentially lose up to 8 pounds and have that fat replaced by muscle. Further studies have shown CLA's uncanny ability to protect against breast cancer and asthma attacks as well as to lower LDL cholesterol, triglyceride, and insulin levels. Because our food supply no longer contains CLA, researchers suggest supplementing with 3,000 milligrams each day.

Consuming too much sugar, carbohydrates, and the wrong fats isn't the only reason some of us gain weight. One of the other factors motivating overeating is depression. That's why I've included another breakthrough supplement on the list: H3 Plus. Procaine-based H3 Plus offers mental health as well as antiaging nutrition, working on the cellular level to allow nutrients to enter and leave the cell. The substance also breaks down in vitamins para-aminobenzoic acid (PABA) and diethyl amino ethanol (DEAE). PABA, a component of folic acid, is vital for cell growth and exercises a hormonelike effect on the system. DEAE is a precursor to neurotransmitters, which help the optimal functioning of the brain.

H3 Plus is based on a successful antiaging and natural antidepressant formula first developed in Romania over fifty years ago. Known as GH3, its dramatic relief was originally documented in a book by Herbert Bailey (please see Bibliography). Now the more bioavailable form is on the market in a convenient tablet. In mere weeks, users experience diminishing depression and a profound new sense of well-being taking its place. And that's good news for weight-loss seekers, because when you feel better emotionally, you are less likely to use food as a reward.

There's even more good news. H3 Plus can also deliver some rather unexpected health and beauty benefits. Seemingly disconnected symptoms noticeably disappear. Achy joints are soothed, because H3 Plus helps improve arthritis; blood pressure normalizes. Collagen is regenerated, producing an appreciable difference in skin, hair, and nail maladies such as acne, rosacea, blotchy skin, age spots, and premature wrinkling. In some cases, hair grows back and even turns darker.

With the nutritional support these health-promoting supplements offer, you'll not only look your best, but you'll feel terrific as well.

SUPPLEMENT	RECOMMENDED DOSAGE
Uni Key Female Formula (copper free)	2 with breakfast, lunch, and dinner
Uni Key Male Formula* (iron free)	1 with breakfast, lunch, and dinner
Uni Key Weight-Loss Formula	2 times daily with meals
Uni Key CLA	1,000 mg/3 times daily before each meal
H3 Plus	1 upon arising and 1 midafternoon

* This supplement can also be used by postmenopausal women.

The following supplements are available at your local health food store:

SUPPLEMENT	RECOMMENDED DOSAGE
Co-Q10	30 mg/3 times daily with meals
L-Carnitine	1,000 mg/2–3 times daily between meals
Neuromin's DHA	200 mg/1–2 times daily with meals

Those of you who are not fish lovers or do not like eating oils, nuts, and seeds should be sure to include these supplements in your dietary regime each day:

SUPPLEMENT	RECOMMENDED DOSAGE
Super MaxEPA	1,000 mg/2–3 times daily with meals
Flaxseed oil	1 tablespoon or 12 capsules daily
Black currant seed oil	90 mg/4 times daily with meals
or Borage oil	1,000 mg/1–3 times daily with meals
or Evening primrose oil	500 mg/4–6 times daily with meals

Note: Essential Woman Oil combines both flaxseed oil and evening primrose oil. This product is available at most health food stores or through Uni Key Health Systems.

CHAPTER SEVEN

THE RECIPES

As we have previously mentioned, a carbohydrate count (CARB ALERT) is given for those recipes in this chapter that have 10 or more carbohydrate grams. Whether you're following the *Eat Fat, Lose Weight* program or just watching carbs in general, keep this in mind when figuring your total carb intake throughout the day.

Breakfast

Start your day off right with an omega-enriched breakfast. It's no contest: Breakfast is the most critical meal of the day. Your body has been without food for approximately twelve hours and needs to be nourished. Eating an omega-enriched breakfast helps rev up your mind, get your energy back in gear, and even out blood sugar levels. Moreover, it fills and satisfies, so you're less likely to hunt out the false energy highs of coffee and sugar-filled breakfast pastries.

If cooking breakfast from scratch isn't your thing, you can still sneak in some healthy omega oils. For example, drizzle a tablespoon of flaxseed oil into some nonfat yogurt just before heading out the door. Or try any of our quick breakfast recipes. Each one is loaded with taste *and* nutrition. In two simple steps, you can whip up a variety of refreshing and filling smoothies, like Peanut Butter Crunch or Berry-Nut. And while the flax is out for your smoothie, it's the perfect time to blend some flax with softened butter. Spread some of this "better butter" on toast for the kids so they get an omega triple-header: support for their immune, cardiovascular, and central nervous systems. The children will also love our warm Oatmeal Flax or Pumpkin Cream Muffins.

Hearty breakfast eaters will enjoy our tempting Heavenly Pancakes, Blueberry Yogurt Flaxjacks, and egg dishes. Please don't shy away from eggs;

contrary to what you may think, eggs are the good guys. A complete source of protein, eggs are packed with vital nutrients, such as vitamins, minerals, amino acids, and antioxidants. And they're high in lecithin, so eggs actually have cholesterol-lowering properties! In fact, studies conducted by the Harvard School of Public Health reveal that eating an egg daily doesn't elevate the risk of heart disease. Plus, eggs satisfy your hunger, and can be made in just a few minutes. We've given you quite a selection, from the Rainbow Veggie Omelet and Zesty-Quick Scramblers to the Easy Seafood Omelet, bound to become a family favorite.

More and more studies reveal the incredible ability of omega-3 oils to improve concentration, enhance feelings of well-being, and reduce aggression. There's really no better way to send yourself to the office or the kids to school than with an omega-rich breakfast.

Smoothies

Within minutes, you can create one of our lip-smacking breakfast smoothies. They're powered up with flax oil to help you start your day the omega way.

PEANUT BUTTER CRUNCH SMOOTHIE*

An unbeatable taste kids—and adults—will love.

MAKES 3 8-OUNCE SERVINGS

1 orange, peeled and seeded
1 cup plain nonfat yogurt
2 tablespoons crunchy peanut butter
2 tablespoons Essential Woman Oil
2 scoops whey protein powder
½ teaspoon nonalcohol vanilla extract
1 cup ice

Step 1. Place ingredients in a blender.

Step 2. Blend until rich and creamy, approximately 2 to 3 minutes.

*CARB ALERT: One serving equals 10 carbohydrate grams.

LUSCIOUS MELON SMOOTHIE*

Delightfully cool and refreshing.

MAKES 3 8-OUNCE SERVINGS

1 cup almond milk
1 cup cantaloupe, cubed
2 tablespoons flax oil
2 scoops whey protein powder
½ teaspoon anise extract
1 cup ice

Step 1. Place ingredients in a blender.

Step 2. Blend until rich and creamy, approximately 2 to 3 minutes.

*CARB ALERT: One serving equals 10 carbohydrate grams.

BERRY-NUT SMOOTHIE*

Fruity and unbelievably delicious.

MAKES 4 8-OUNCE SERVINGS

1 cup frozen blueberries
¼ cup frozen strawberries
1¾ cups spring water
4 tablespoons nonfat plain yogurt
2 tablespoons flax oil
2 tablespoons almond butter
2 scoops whey protein powder
1 cup ice

Step 1. Place ingredients in a blender.

Step 2. Blend until rich and creamy, approximately 2 to 3 minutes.

*CARB ALERT: One serving equals 10 carbohydrate grams.

PINEAPPLE-PECAN SMOOTHIE*

The sweetness of the tropics takes a nutty turn.

MAKES 2 8-OUNCE SERVINGS

⅓ cup almond milk
¼ cup nonfat plain yogurt
1 cup spring water
8 pecans
1 cup chunk pineapple
2 tablespoons flax oil
2 scoops whey protein powder
1 cup ice

Step 1. Place ingredients in a blender.

Step 2. Blend until rich and creamy, approximately 2 to 3 minutes.

*CARB ALERT: One serving equals 20 carbohydrate grams.

PACIFIC COAST SMOOTHIE*

A sweet and healthy combo that can't be beat!

MAKES 3 8-OUNCE SERVINGS

½ cup avocado, cubed
5 pitted dates
4 tablespoons nonfat plain yogurt
2 tablespoons flax oil
2 scoops whey protein powder
¼ cup chunk pineapple
1¾ cups spring water
1 cup ice

Step 1. Place ingredients in a blender.

Step 2. Blend until rich and creamy, approximately 2 to 3 minutes.

*CARB ALERT: One serving equals 16 carbohydrate grams.

ARCTIC SMOOTHIE*

Refreshing, exhilarating, absolutely delicious!

MAKES 3 8-OUNCE SERVINGS

2 cups pitted fresh cherries (approximately 24 cherries)
1 cup nonfat plain yogurt
2 tablespoons Essential Woman Oil
2 scoops whey protein powder
¼ teaspoon nonalcohol mint extract
½ cup cranapple juice
1 cup ice

Step 1. Place ingredients in a blender.

Step 2. Blend until rich and creamy, approximately 2 to 3 minutes.

*CARB ALERT: One serving equals 22 carbohydrate grams.

RAZZ-BERRY SMOOTHIE*

A snappy morning treat.

MAKES 4 8-OUNCE SERVINGS

1¼ cups frozen raspberries
¾ cup cranberry juice
1 cup spring water
4 tablespoons nonfat plain yogurt
2 tablespoons flax oil
2 tablespoons almond butter
2 scoops whey protein powder
1 cup ice

Step 1. Place ingredients in a blender.

Step 2. Blend until creamy, approximately 2 minutes.

*CARB ALERT: One serving equals 11 carbohydrate grams.

Breads, Muffins, and Pancakes

You don't have to give up these delicious comfort foods. We've got some mouthwatering, easy-to-make recipes your whole family will enjoy. And naturally, they're made with fabulous flax to give you a healthy omega-3 boost.

FLAX-FOR-THOUGHT BREAD*

Just like Mom's—only better. This delicious quick-bread recipe is a spin-off of Jade Beutler's version, published in his Flax for Life *cookbook.*

MAKES 6 SMALL LOAVES

> 2 eggs
> ½ cup raw honey
>   Juice of 2 lemons, with enough buttermilk added
>   to make 1½ cups
> 1 teaspoon sea salt
> 2 teaspoons baking soda
> 2 cups ground flaxseed (flour consistency)
> 1 cup whole wheat or spelt flour
> 1 cup all-purpose flour
>   Grated lemon peel (from 2 lemons)

Step 1. Preheat oven to 325°F. Lightly oil six 3 × 7-inch bread pans.

Step 2. Combine liquid ingredients (eggs, raw honey, lemon juice, and buttermilk) in a mixing bowl.

Step 3. Mix dry ingredients (including grated lemon peel), and blend them into the liquid mixture.

Step 4. Pour batter evenly into six bread pans and bake for 45 minutes or until a toothpick inserted in the center comes out clean.

HEALTHY FUN TWIST: Add ½ cup chopped walnuts to the dry ingredients. For those not counting carbs, try adding 1 cup currants, raisins, chopped dates, or chopped prunes in Step 3 above. (Be sure to soak dried fruit for a few minutes to soften, then drain before using.)

*CARB ALERT: One loaf equals 36 carbohydrate grams.

KORNY MUFFINS*

Let the kids grab one of these terrific muffins for a change of pace.

MAKES 12 MUFFINS

1 tablespoon extra-virgin olive oil
1 medium-sized white onion, minced
1 cup corn kernels, from cob or canned
1 large garlic clove, pressed
½ teaspoon fresh basil, chopped
Pinch of salt
1 egg
3 tablespoons honey
¾ cup rice milk
¼ cup high-oleic safflower oil
1 cup stone-ground cornmeal
½ cup whole wheat pastry flour
2 teaspoons baking powder

Step 1. Preheat oven to 375°F. Place paper baking cups in 2½-inch muffin tins.

Step 2. In a skillet, warm the olive oil and sauté onion.

Step 3. Add corn, garlic, basil, and salt, sautéing for 2 minutes until seasonings are well blended. Set aside and let cool.

Step 4. Meanwhile, in a small bowl, whisk egg, honey, rice milk, and safflower oil. Then stir in onion-corn mixture.

Step 5. In a large bowl, mix cornmeal, flour, and baking powder. Blend in onion-corn-egg mixture.

Step 6. Fill bake cups with batter ¾ full. Bake for approximately 25 minutes or until a toothpick inserted in the center comes out clean.

*CARB ALERT: One serving equals 15 carbohydrate grams.

OATMEAL FLAX MUFFINS*

In a hurry? These nutty muffins make a tasty quick meal or nutritious snack.

MAKES 12 MUFFINS

1 **egg**
1 **cup raw steel-cut oats**
¾ **cup rice milk**
⅓ **cup honey**
½ **cup high-oleic safflower oil**
1 **cup whole wheat pastry flour**
2 **tablespoons flaxmeal**
3 **teaspoons baking powder**
1 **teaspoon cinnamon**
1 **teaspoon nutmeg**
⅓ **cup crushed walnuts, coarsely chopped**

Step 1. Preheat oven to 350°F and place paper baking cups in 2½-inch muffin tins.

Step 2. Whisk egg in a large bowl and blend with oats, rice milk, honey, and oil.

Step 3. In separate bowl, mix flour, flaxmeal, baking powder, and spices.

Step 4. Gradually blend flour mixture into the oat mixture—*using just a few strokes.*

Step 5. Spoon batter evenly into muffin tins, topping with chopped walnuts. Bake for approximately 15 minutes or until a toothpick inserted in the center comes out clean.

*CARB ALERT: One serving equals 18 carbohydrate grams.

PUMPKIN CREAM MUFFINS

So luscious and light, everyone will be singing your praises!

MAKES 6 MUFFINS

- ¼ cup soy flour
- ¼ cup ground pumpkin seeds
- 3 tablespoons nonfat plain yogurt
- 2 tablespoons butter, melted
- ½ teaspoon baking powder
- 2 large eggs, lightly beaten

Step 1. Preheat oven to 350°F and grease six 2½-inch muffin tins.

Step 2. Combine all ingredients in a food processor, blending until smooth.

Step 3. Spoon mixture evenly into muffin tins, filling halfway. (Pour water into empty muffin cups.)

Step 4. Bake for approximately 20 to 25 minutes or until a toothpick inserted in the center comes out clean. Let cool before serving.

HEAVENLY PANCAKES*

These pancakes are out of this world. They're made with both soy flour and omega-3–rich flax flour to help balance carbs.

MAKES 4 SERVINGS (2 PANCAKES = 1 SERVING)

- ½ cup soy flour
- ¼ cup whole wheat flour
- ¼ cup stone-ground cornmeal
- 2 teaspoons baking powder
- ½ teaspoon salt
- 2½ teaspoons flax flour
- 1 egg, separated
- 1 cup rice milk
- 1 teaspoon high-oleic safflower oil

Step 1. Combine dry ingredients in a small bowl and set aside.

Step 2. Beat egg white until stiff.

Step 3. In a large bowl, beat egg yolk and rice milk together. Gradually add in dry ingredients.

Step 4. Gently fold in beaten egg white.

Step 5. Pour oil into a medium skillet and heat. Pour pancake batter on skillet, turning when bubbly. Cook on low temperature because cooking with soy flour causes food to brown faster than usual.

Step 6. Lightly top with fruit jam or 100 percent maple syrup blended with flax oil for the kids or 1 teaspoon flax oil for you; serve warm.

*CARB ALERT: One serving equals 15 carbohydrate grams. If you're counting carbs, you may want to substitute water for the rice milk.

BLUEBERRY YOGURT FLAXJACKS*

Made with soy and flax flour, these light and fluffy pancakes have reduced carbs.

MAKES 4 SERVINGS (2 FLAXJACKS = 1 SERVING)

1 egg
1 tablespoon high-oleic safflower oil
¾ cup rice milk or water
1½ cups nonfat plain yogurt
3 tablespoons flax flour
⅔ cup soy flour
½ cup spelt flour
1 teaspoon baking soda
⅛ teaspoon sea salt
¼ cup blueberries
1 tablespoon high-oleic safflower oil

Step 1. Beat egg, oil, rice milk or water, and yogurt in a small bowl.

Step 2. Mix dry ingredients in a separate, large bowl.

Step 3. Add egg mixture to dry ingredients, and stir in blueberries.

Step 4. Pour the remaining tablespoon of oil into a medium skillet and heat. Cook on low temperature, because cooking with soy flour causes food to brown faster than usual.

Step 5. Using ⅓ cup of flaxjack mixture for each serving (2 flaxjacks), pour batter into heated skillet.

Step 6. Flip flaxjacks over when batter bubbles.

Step 7. Serve warm; lightly top with 100 percent maple syrup, if desired.

*CARB ALERT: One serving equals 23 carbohydrate grams.

Eggs

The egg is back! It's healthy, it's rich in protein, and it contains the beautifying sulfur-based amino acids essential for luxurious hair, healthy nails, and radiant skin.

THE EGGS-ACT FACTS

- Eggs should be cooked so whites are firm and yolks are just starting to firm up.
- Egg-white (ropelike) strands are safe to eat and indicate a fresh egg.
- Eggs should be refrigerated in their original carton and used within three weeks of purchase.
- Eggs with blood spots are safe to eat: Simply remove the spot with a knife tip.
- An egg yolk has up to 45 percent of the egg's protein as well as most of its vitamins and minerals.

ZESTY-QUICK SCRAMBLERS

Start your day with a little kick.

MAKES 2 SERVINGS

4 eggs
2 large garlic cloves, pressed
1 teaspoon fresh oregano, chopped
½ teaspoon fresh basil, chopped
  Pinch of cayenne pepper
  Salt to taste
2–3 scallions, finely chopped
1 tablespoon extra-virgin olive oil

Step 1. Whisk eggs in a medium bowl with spices.

Step 2. Stir in scallions.

Step 3. Pour the olive oil in medium skillet and heat.

Step 4. Pour in egg mixture and scramble with spatula, cooking until done.

PEPPER AND ONION SCRAMBLE

Delicious with a side of sliced tomato and your favorite seasonings.

MAKES 2 SERVINGS

4 eggs
2 large garlic cloves, pressed
1 teaspoon fresh oregano, chopped
  Salt and pepper to taste
1 large green bell pepper, diced
½ large white onion, diced
2 teaspoons olive or high-oleic safflower oil
½ cup grated cheddar cheese

Step 1. Whisk eggs and spices in a medium bowl.

Step 2. Stir in green pepper and onion.

Step 3. Lightly coat a medium skillet with oil and heat.

Step 4. Pour egg mixture into skillet. Sprinkle in cheese, then scramble and cook until done.

ONE-TWO-THREE HUEVOS RANCHEROS

A Southwest breakfast adaptation.

MAKES 2 SERVINGS

1 cup Pico de Gallo (page 67)
4 eggs
  Salt and pepper to taste

Step 1. Warm Pico de Gallo sauce in a large skillet.

Step 2. When the sauce begins to simmer, add the eggs and seasoning, then scramble.

Step 3. Dish onto plates and top with additional sauce.

SOME-LIKE-IT-HOT POACHED EGGS

A good-looking presentation—and scrumptious, too!

MAKES 2 SERVINGS

4 eggs
1 small garlic clove, pressed
¼ teaspoon fresh basil, chopped
Sprinkle of cayenne pepper
Salt to taste
2 slices whole grain toast
2 tablespoons Essential Woman Oil
Parsley sprigs, for garnish

Step 1. Crack eggs individually into poacher cups.

Step 2. Sprinkle an even amount of spices over each one. (Lightly tap the side of the measuring spoon over each egg.)

Step 3. Follow directions for poacher, or cook for around 3 minutes for soft eggs.

Step 4. While eggs are cooking, toast 2 slices of whole grain bread and cut each slice in half.

Step 5. Top each half slice of toast with ½ tablespoon Essential Woman Oil, poached egg, and garnish.

HEALTHY FUN TWIST: Place a strip of lox with a razor-thin slice of tomato and onion on each piece of toast before topping with seasoned poached egg.

OREGANO

Used by the ancient Greeks, this mint-family herb is packed with antioxidant power. It's been used to help relieve headaches, sinus infections, coughs, indigestion, and menstrual problems, as well as arthritis, emphysema, body odor, and high blood pressure.

RAINBOW VEGGIE OMELET

Mornings will seem a little brighter with this deliciously colorful meal.

MAKES 2 SERVINGS

4	eggs
¾	teaspoon fresh parsley, chopped
2	large garlic cloves, pressed
1	teaspoon fresh oregano, chopped
	Salt to taste
	Pinch of cayenne (optional)
1	tablespoon extra-virgin olive oil
¼	large green bell pepper, chopped
¼	large red bell pepper, chopped
¼	large yellow bell pepper, chopped
¼	large orange bell pepper, chopped
2	small shallots, chopped
1–2	celery stalks, minced
¼	cup mushrooms, finely chopped
¼	cup tomatoes, finely chopped
⅛	cup black olives, chopped

Step 1. Whisk eggs in a medium bowl with seasonings; set aside.

Step 2. Pour olive oil in skillet and warm. Add peppers, shallots, celery, mushrooms, tomatoes, and olives.

Step 3. Sauté for about 1 minute, then pour in egg mixture.

Step 4. As the bottom side of the omelet sets, raise the omelet's edge to help the uncooked portion on top run into the cooked egg. When cooked, grasp the skillet handle with one hand, then gently roll the omelet onto a plate using a spatula.

EASY SEAFOOD OMELET

Got seafood leftovers? Toss 'em in for an extra-special morning delight.

MAKES 2 SERVINGS

4	eggs
2	large garlic cloves, pressed
¾	teaspoon fresh basil, chopped
¼	teaspoon fresh dill, chopped
	Salt and pepper to taste
1–2	celery stalks, minced
¼	cup tomatoes, finely chopped
2	scallions, finely chopped
¼	cup mushrooms, finely chopped
½	cup chopped, cooked shrimp, crab, or scallops (or combination)
1	tablespoon extra-virgin olive oil
1–2	sprigs fresh parsley, for garnish

Step 1. Whisk eggs and spices in a small bowl.

Step 2. Stir in chopped vegetables and cooked seafood.

Step 3. Pour olive oil into an omelet pan or nonstick skillet with sloping sides and heat.

Step 4. Pour egg mixture into the skillet.

Step 5. As the bottom side of the omelet sets, raise the omelet's edge to help the top uncooked portion run under to the cooked side. When cooked, grasp the skillet handle with one hand, then gently roll the omelet onto a plate using a spatula. Garnish with fresh parsley.

HELPFUL HINT: If you don't have shrimp, crab, or scallop leftovers, you can sauté your favorite seafood for a few minutes in the skillet beforehand. While it's cooking, do Steps 1 through 3. Then pour the egg mixture (Step 4) into the skillet with the cooked seafood, lightly blending. Complete by following Step 5.

GREEN GODDESS FRITTATA

For breakfast or brunch, this is one big, green, nutritious pleaser.

MAKES 4 SERVINGS

6 eggs, beaten
½ cup nonfat cottage cheese
1½ cups fresh or frozen chopped spinach
2 green onions, minced
1 teaspoon ground cumin
2 large garlic cloves, pressed
Salt to taste
1 teaspoon butter

Step 1. Preheat oven to 350°F.

Step 2. Combine eggs, cottage cheese, spinach, onions, and seasonings.

Step 3. Melt butter in a large skillet and add egg mixture.

Step 4. Cook over medium heat on stovetop for 3 minutes.

Step 5. Place in oven and bake for another 10 minutes or until egg mixture sets.

Sensational Starters

Omegasizing any meal is a snap with these delectable dips, pestos, pâtés, salsas, and tasty tidbits. We've purposely "fattened up" this section as a great way to introduce a wide variety of healthy alternatives. Everyone (especially kids!) loves nibbling while waiting for the main meal. But instead of reaching for potato chips and dips laden with unhealthy fats, try one of the irresistible recipes included in this section. They can all be made in a few minutes—a big plus in today's forever-on-the-go lifestyle. And you can savor each morsel without the worry of consuming the unhealthy oils typically found in commercial dips and dressings.

We've used omega-rich flaxseed oil and extra-virgin olive oil. Savory spices are also included for their immune-boosting power as well as intriguing seafood combinations to make your taste buds spin with delight. Wait until you taste our Avocado-Cilantro Dip; mouthwatering hummus recipes from around the globe; Tangy Tapenade made with walnuts, green and black olives, and capers; our titillating array of pestos and salsas, such as

Paradise Salsa blended with bell peppers, ginger, and fresh mint; not to mention our crowd-pleasing hors d'oeuvres such as Hotsy-Totsy Shrimp Cocktail and Spinach-Walnut Stuffed Mushrooms.

Any of these mouthwatering starters can be made ahead of time and served in a jiffy. That can be extremely helpful when you've got a hungry family at your heels or some unexpected guests at your door. Sensational starters are also wonderful icebreakers. They're a delicious way to pass the time, chitchatting with old friends, meeting new neighbors, entertaining business associates, or getting reacquainted with your busy family. Bon appetit!

Dips

Take the plunge. Grab your favorite veggies and dip into these delectable crowd-pleasers. They're one of the easiest ways to get your family to eat those healthy omega fats.

AVOCADO-CILANTRO DIP

Family won't eat veggies? Serve this tasty dip with some crunchy jicama, carrots, cucumbers, or celery cut into sticks. Then stand back and watch those veggies disappear!

MAKES 1 CUP OR 2 SERVINGS

  1 **large ripe avocado, peeled, pitted, and diced**
 ¼ **cup scallions, finely chopped**
 ¼ **cup fresh cilantro, stemmed**
  1 **tablespoon fresh lemon juice**
  2 **medium tomatoes, seeded and finely chopped**
 ½ **teaspoon ground cumin**
2–3 **drops of hot sauce, such as Tabasco**
     Salt to taste
  1 **tablespoon flax oil**

Step 1. Place avocado in a large bowl and mash.

Step 2. Blend in scallions, cilantro, lemon juice, tomatoes, cumin, hot sauce, and salt.

Step 3. Pour in oil and blend, using a wooden spoon.

Step 4. Serve with veggie dippers.

MIDDLE EASTERN HUMMUS*

Conjure up the magic of 1,001 Arabian nights . . . but with an omega twist. Use as a veggie dip or as a spread on grilled fish.

MAKES 1¼ CUPS OR 5 SERVINGS

1 15-ounce can chickpeas, drained
⅛ cup tahini
3 tablespoons fresh lemon juice
3 tablespoons flax oil
1 large garlic clove, minced
¼ teaspoon ground cumin
   Dash of cayenne
2 tablespoons fresh parsley, chopped, for garnish
1 lemon, cut in wedges, for garnish

Step 1. Combine first six ingredients in a blender or food processor, blending until mixture turns to a paste. Add water if needed.

Step 2. Transfer to a serving bowl and sprinkle with a dash of cayenne.

Step 3. Garnish with parsley and lemon wedges.

*CARB ALERT: One serving equals 11 carbohydrate grams.

MEDITERRANEAN HUMMUS*

A timeless pleasure made with a flavorful blend of spices.

MAKES 1¼ CUPS OR 5 SERVINGS

1 15-ounce can cannellini beans, drained
3 tablespoons fresh lemon juice
3 tablespoons flax oil
1 large garlic clove, minced
¼ teaspoon dried oregano
¼ cup fresh basil, chopped
2 tablespoons fresh parsley, chopped, for garnish
1 lemon, cut in wedges, for garnish

Step 1. Process first five ingredients in a blender or food processor until mixture turns to a paste. Add water if needed.

Step 2. Transfer to a serving bowl and stir in fresh basil.

Step 3. Garnish with parsley and lemon wedges.

*CARB ALERT: One serving equals 11 carbohydrate grams.

CAYENNE

Used for centuries throughout South America and Africa, this remarkable herb has a brilliant red hue and packs quite a bite. It has the uncanny ability to halt pain impulses, making it an ideal ingredient in remedies to combat muscle pain, arthritis, shingles, cluster headaches, and foot pain. Cayenne is also used to reduce blood pressure and ensure a healthy heart as well as to aid digestion.

CARIBBEAN HUMMUS

A peanutty spin-off your family will adore. Serve it with raw vegetables or toasted corn tortillas.

MAKES 1¼ CUPS OR 5 SERVINGS

7 ounces cooked chickpeas
7 ounces cooked black beans
3 tablespoons fresh lemon juice
3 tablespoons flax oil
1 large garlic clove, minced
¼ teaspoon ground cumin
¼ cup fresh cilantro, stemmed
Dash of cayenne
¼ cup roasted peanuts
2 tablespoons fresh cilantro, chopped, for garnish
1 tablespoon roasted peanuts, chopped, for topping

Step 1. Process first eight ingredients in a blender or food processor until mixture turns to paste. Add water if needed.

Step 2. Transfer to a serving bowl and blend in ¼ cup peanuts.

Step 3. Garnish with chopped cilantro and sprinkle with chopped peanuts.

EGGPLANT TAPENADE

A spectacularly easy dip for your favorite veggie sticks; try celery, jicama, carrots, zucchini, or broccoli florets.

MAKES 2 CUPS

1 large eggplant
2 tablespoons extra-virgin olive oil
¼ cup onion
¼ cup fresh basil, chopped
¼ cup fresh parsley, chopped
2 large garlic cloves, pressed
Juice of ½ lemon
Salt and pepper to taste

Step 1. Preheat oven to 400°F. Place eggplant on baking sheet and roast until soft and skin is blackened, approximately 30 minutes. Remove from oven and let cool.

Step 2. Cut eggplant in half lengthwise. Using a spoon, scrape pulp from skin and place in a food processor.

Step 3. Add olive oil, onion, basil, parsley, garlic, and lemon juice; then blend into a paste. Add salt and pepper to taste.

TANGY TAPENADE

Try this flavorful blend on grilled poultry or fish, a hamburger . . . and, of course, with raw veggies.

MAKES 1 CUP

⅛ cup black olives, chopped
⅛ cup green olives with pimientos, drained, pitted, and chopped
⅛ cup capers, drained
¼ cup walnuts, chopped
½ cup fresh basil, chopped
2 large garlic cloves, pressed
½ cup extra-virgin olive oil
2 tablespoons fresh lemon juice
Salt and pepper to taste

Step 1. Combine all ingredients in a food processor and pulse, lightly blending. Do not purée.

Step 2. Transfer to a small bowl and refrigerate until serving.

BASIL-FLAX AIOLI

An absolute classic. Delicious as a dip or as a spread on fish and poultry.

MAKES 1¼ CUPS OR 5 SERVINGS

> 1 cup Spectrum Naturals organic mayonnaise
> 1 tablespoon flax oil
> 1 tablespoon virgin or extra-virgin olive oil
> 4 garlic cloves, minced
> ⅛ teaspoon crushed red pepper flakes
> ¼ cup fresh basil, chopped
> Salt and pepper to taste

Step 1. Blend mayonnaise and flaxseed oil in a small bowl and set aside.

Step 2. In a small skillet, heat olive oil and sauté garlic until golden. Then add crushed red pepper.

Step 3. Let garlic mixture cool, then add to mayonnaise–flaxseed oil mixture.

Step 4. Blend in basil and season to taste.

Step 5. Chill in refrigerator.

Pestos

Pestos provide Old World flavors with a twenty-first-century spin. Our pestos give you the zest—plus the omega richness needed for a healthy diet. No matter which one you try, it's bound to be a smash hit.

OMEGA STAR PESTO

Just the right touch for fish; try it on the Grilled Tuna Steaks (featured on page 132).

MAKES ½ CUP

> 4 garlic cloves, pressed
> ½ cup fresh basil, stemmed

¼ cup walnuts

2 tablespoons black olives, minced

¼ cup sun-dried tomatoes with their oil

1 tablespoon virgin or extra-virgin olive oil

Step 1. Place garlic, basil, walnuts, olives, and sun-dried tomatoes with oil reserved in a food processor.

Step 2. With motor running, add reserved oil from tomatoes (approximately ½ tablespoon) and 1 tablespoon olive oil.

Step 3. Scrape down sides of processor's bowl as needed, and process until a paste is formed.

THAT'S ITALIAN PESTO

Absolutely perfecto for our Spring Minestrone soup on page 80. Just top each bowl with a tablespoon of pesto—and enjoy!

MAKES ½ CUP

2 garlic cloves

1 cup packed fresh basil leaves

4 tablespoons virgin or extra-virgin olive oil

6 tablespoons pine nuts

4 tablespoons Parmesan cheese

Step 1. Place all ingredients in a food processor.

Step 2. Process until a paste is formed, scraping down the sides of processor's bowl as needed.

THAT'S NUTS!

Those irresistible pine nuts (pignoli) seem to charm their way into cuisine throughout the Mediterranean. They're in pesto, jams, rice dishes, and stuffings. Italians serve them with sardines, spinach, and swordfish. In Spain, pine nuts are tossed into chicken or rabbit dishes.

Pâtés

You don't have to be a gourmet cook to make these simple pâtés—but everyone just might think you are. Serve them at a party, club meeting, or intimate dinner for two. Then keep an ear out for that inevitable round of applause.

PARTY PÂTÉ

Keep them guessing. Only you'll know this pâté is nutritious as well as delicious.

MAKES 3 CUPS

2 13-ounce cans salmon packed in water, drained, skinned, and deboned
1 8-ounce can smoked oysters
1 2-ounce can anchovy fillets, well rinsed and drained
1 garlic clove, pressed
2 tablespoons fresh arugula, chopped
2 tablespoons fresh cilantro, chopped
1 teaspoon fennel seed
1 teaspoon horseradish
1 tablespoon fresh lime juice
¼ cup fresh parsley, minced
3 tablespoons capers
   Lemon wedges, for garnish

Step 1. Place first nine ingredients in a food processor. Press the off/on button every 5 to 7 seconds to avoid overprocessing. If the mixture sticks to the sides of the bowl, scrape down with spatula.

Step 2. Mix in parsley and capers.

Step 3. Put mixture in a glass loaf pan and refrigerate for at least 4 hours.

Step 4. Before serving, invert loaf and serve on platter. Garnish with lemon wedges.

TUNA PÂTÉ

The sun-dried tomatoes are the secret ingredient.

MAKES 12 APPETIZERS

8 ounces canned solid white tuna packed in water, drained
⅛ cup fresh lemon juice
¼ cup scallions, chopped
½ cup Spectrum Naturals organic mayonnaise
¼ cup sun-dried tomatoes, finely chopped
⅛ cup fresh basil, chopped
Salt and pepper to taste
12 basil leaves
12 baguette slices, or 12 cucumber slices
Lemon slices, cut paper thin

Step 1. Place tuna in a large bowl and mash with a fork.

Step 2. Stir in lemon juice, scallions, mayonnaise, sun-dried tomatoes, basil, salt, and pepper.

Step 3. Mix until a spreadable consistency.

Step 4. Place a basil leaf on each baguette or cucumber slice.

Step 5. Top each with pâté, and garnish with lemon wedges.

Salsas

Give your meals some pizzazz with one of America's most popular condiments—salsa. We've given it an omega twist with the help of flax oil. Try any one of these stupendous salsas on grilled meats, fish, or poultry. Or spoon some on your favorite egg or vegetable dishes.

PICO DE GALLO*

This tomato-based relish is a staple in most Latin American countries. Try it over grilled meats, poultry, fish, or even vegetables.

MAKES 2 CUPS OR 4 SERVINGS

2½ pounds roma tomatoes, seeded and finely chopped
 1   large red onion, finely chopped
 ¾   cup fresh cilantro, chopped
 3   jalapeño peppers, seeded and minced
 1   teaspoon chili powder
 3   tablespoons fresh lime juice
 3   tablespoons extra-virgin olive oil
     Salt and pepper to taste

Step 1. Combine all ingredients in a bowl, seasoning with salt and pepper.

Step 2. Cover and marinate for 1 hour.

*CARB ALERT: One serving equals 11 carbohydrate grams.

TOMATO-BASIL SALSA

Expand your repertoire with this sassy Mediterranean number. Molto buono!

MAKES 2 CUPS

 ¼   cup sun-dried tomatoes, chopped
 2   cups plum tomatoes, seeded and chopped
 2   tablespoons black olives, chopped
 2   tablespoons fresh basil, chopped
 1   anchovy fillet, drained, rinsed, and chopped
 1   tablespoon extra-virgin olive oil
 1   tablespoon apple cider vinegar

2 garlic cloves, pressed
1 teaspoon capers, drained
  Salt and pepper to taste

Step 1. Place all ingredients in a bowl, using salt and pepper to taste.

Step 2. Refrigerate and allow flavors to blend.

PARADISE SALSA

A zesty treat you can make in one easy step. Serve it with any of your favorite grilled dishes.

MAKES 1¼ CUPS

½ papaya, peeled, pitted, and cut into small cubes
½ red bell pepper, slivered
5 tablespoons fresh lime juice
1 teaspoon fresh ginger, grated
½ teaspoon crushed red pepper flakes
1 teaspoon fresh mint, chopped
2 tablespoons flax oil
  Salt and pepper to taste

Mix all ingredients in a bowl and marinate for at least 2 hours.

BLACK BEAN AND PEANUT SALSA*

Bursting with flavor. A crunchy delight to accompany hors d'oeuvres or to top your favorite meat, such as the Cuban-Style Turkey Breast on page 147.

MAKES 2 CUPS OR 4 SERVINGS

1 15-ounce can black beans, drained and rinsed
⅓ cup fresh or canned corn kernels
¼ cup peanuts
¼ cup green onions, chopped
½ cup cilantro, chopped
3 tablespoons fresh lime juice
1–1½ tablespoons extra-virgin olive oil
  Salt and pepper to taste

Step 1. Place all ingredients in a large bowl and lightly toss.

Step 2. Cover and allow to stand for up to 1 hour.

*CARB ALERT: One serving equals 17 carbohydrate grams.

Tasty Tidbits

Get the conversation started with these enticing, omega-rich nibblers. They're excellent as hors d'oeuvres or snacks. Whichever way you use them, everyone will be singing your praises.

EGGPLANT AND SMOKED SALMON TOPPERS

Planning a party? Here's a quick appetizer your guests will enjoy.

MAKES 4 SERVINGS

2 teaspoons extra-virgin olive oil
1 large eggplant, cut lengthwise into 4 slices
2 tablespoons extra-virgin olive oil
2 tablespoons balsamic vinegar
1 tablespoon dried oregano
1 tablespoon dried rosemary
½ pound smoked salmon, cut into 4 strips
2 tablespoons capers, drained
2 tablespoons black olives, chopped
1 tablespoon fresh dill, chopped

Step 1. Preheat broiler. Then oil a large baking sheet with the olive oil.

Step 2. Brush eggplant slices on both sides with olive oil and balsamic vinegar.

Step 3. Sprinkle each with oregano and rosemary.

Step 4. Place in broiler and broil, about 5 minutes per side.

Step 5. Allow to cool and place on serving plate.

Step 6. Top each slice with salmon strips, and sprinkle with capers, olives, and dill.

SPINACH-WALNUT-STUFFED MUSHROOMS

Crunchy and delectable.

MAKES 12 MUSHROOMS

3 teaspoons extra-virgin olive oil
1 10-ounce package frozen spinach, thawed and drained
¼ cup chopped walnuts
1 egg yolk
1 teaspoon fresh tarragon, chopped
   Salt and pepper to taste
12 large white mushrooms, cleaned and stemmed

Step 1. Heat oven to 350°F. Grease a small cookie sheet with 2 teaspoons oil.

Step 2. In a large bowl, mix remaining teaspoon oil with spinach, walnuts, egg yolk, and tarragon; season to taste.

Step 3. Stuff each mushroom with spinach mixture and place on cookie sheet.

Step 4. Bake for 15 to 25 minutes or until mixture is firm to the touch. Serve hot.

SAUSAGE-STUFFED MUSHROOMS

Hearty taste . . . a meal in itself.

MAKES 12 MUSHROOMS

12 large fresh mushrooms, cleaned with stems reserved
2 tablespoons extra-virgin olive oil
¼ cup red onion, chopped
2 garlic cloves, pressed
¼ pound ground turkey sausage
¼ teaspoon cinnamon
½ teaspoon anise seed
   Salt and pepper to taste
¼ cup walnuts, ground to a flourlike consistency
3 tablespoons flax flour
½ cup Chicken Stock (page 77)
   Parmesan cheese, for topping

Step 1. Preheat oven to 350°F.

Step 2. Chop mushroom stems.

Step 3. Pour 1 tablespoon olive oil into skillet and sauté onions until translucent.

Step 4. Add mushroom stems and garlic to skillet. Sauté, then transfer to a bowl.

Step 5. Pour 1 tablespoon olive oil into skillet and cook the ground turkey sausage.

Step 6. Stir in the cinnamon and anise seed. Season with salt and pepper.

Step 7. Transfer to bowl with mushroom stems.

Step 8. Blend in walnuts and flaxseed flour.

Step 9. Stuff each mushroom with the sausage mixture.

Step 10. Place mushrooms on a baking sheet and drizzle with chicken broth. Place in oven and cook for 20 to 30 minutes. Sprinkle with Parmesan cheese and serve warm.

SEASIDE DEVILED EGGS

Our yummy take on an old-time favorite.

MAKES 4 SERVINGS

4 large hard-boiled eggs
1 5-ounce can solid white tuna packed in water, drained
1 tablespoon fresh chives, chopped
2 teaspoons capers, drained and chopped
1 tablespoon Spectrum Naturals organic mayonnaise
Salt and pepper to taste
Paprika, for garnish

Step 1. Cut eggs in half lengthwise.

Step 2. Scoop out egg yolks and place in a medium bowl.

Step 3. Mash yolks with a fork.

Step 4. Chop two egg-white halves and mix in with yolks.

Step 5. Add tuna, chives, and capers to mixture.

Step 6. Blend in mayonnaise and mix well. Season to taste.

Step 7. Spoon about 1 tablespoonful into each egg half. Shape and sprinkle with paprika.

Step 8. Place on a serving plate, cover, and chill.

HOTSY-TOTSY SHRIMP COCKTAIL

Jalapeño peppers and chili powder turn up the heat.

MAKES 4 SERVINGS

1½ cups Clamato juice
¼ cup dry vermouth
2 tablespoons fresh cilantro, finely chopped
1 jalapeño pepper, cut in half
1 pound cooked shrimp, peeled, deveined, and cut in half
3 tablespoons flax oil
6 tomatillos, husks removed, chopped
1 medium tomato, seeded and chopped
1 small red onion, chopped
1 tablespoon fresh cilantro, chopped
1 teaspoon fresh lime juice
½ teaspoon chili powder
Salt and pepper to taste
1 lemon, quartered, for garnish

Step 1. Combine first four ingredients in a medium saucepan and heat to a boil.

Step 2. Strain liquid and allow to cool.

Step 3. Add shrimp, oil, tomatillos, tomato, onion, cilantro, lime juice, and chili powder to sauce. Season to taste.

Step 4. Refrigerate until chilled. Serve in a glass bowl with lemon garnish.

SHRIMP REMOULADE

Capture the heart of New Orleans. This Creole dish will easily become a favorite.

MAKES 4 SERVINGS

⅓ cup fresh parsley, coarsely chopped
½ celery stalk, chopped
1 garlic clove, pressed
¼ cup Dijon mustard
1 tablespoon creamy horseradish
¼ cup Spectrum Naturals organic mayonnaise
½ teaspoon Tabasco sauce
½ teaspoon Worcestershire sauce
¼ cup flax oil
2 cups romaine lettuce, shredded
1 pound cooked shrimp, peeled, deveined, and chopped
Salt and pepper to taste

Step 1. Combine first three ingredients in a large bowl.

Step 2. Blend in mustard, horseradish, and mayonnaise.

Step 3. Add Tabasco and Worcestershire sauces.

Step 4. Slowly whisk in the oil.

Step 5. Place lettuce and shrimp in bowl and coat with mixture, seasoning to taste.

Step 6. Cool in the refrigerator and serve chilled.

MORE ABOUT NUTS

Toasted or fried cashews blended with coconut add a savory spark to meals in southern India, while in the north, the ancient nutty delights of Mogul emperors (pistachios and almonds) continue to make their mark. From pilafs and puddings to meat entrées, natives toast, grind, or sliver their way to culinary bliss.

SPICY NUTS

Quick, easy, and delicious.

MAKES 1 CUP

1 tablespoon peanut oil
¼ cup walnuts
¼ cup cashews
¼ cup pepitas or pumpkin seeds
¼ cup almonds
1 tablespoon maple syrup
¼ teaspoon stevia (optional)
1 tablespoon chili powder
1 teaspoon allspice
Dash of cayenne pepper

Step 1. Preheat oven to 350°F. Oil a large baking sheet with peanut oil.

Step 2. Place nuts and seeds in a large bowl and mix.

Step 3. Blend in remaining ingredients.

Step 4. Spread in a single layer on sheet and bake until toasted, about 15 minutes.

Step 5. Remove from oven, cool, and serve.

Savory Soups and Stupendous Stews

Family stressed out? Let 'em eat—soup! It's a well-known fact that soup has an uncanny way of pushing away the blues and making you feel all warm and cozy inside. Of course, most soups on the market are loaded with unhealthy fats, too much salt, and sometimes even sugar. But we've got a healthy solution for you: a number of family-pleasing soups and stews you can easily make from scratch. And when they're created with flax oil, they are even better for you. Tantalize your taste buds with longtime favorites such as Hearty Chicken Vegetable, Mushroom Barley, and Spring Minestrone. Or experiment with Thai Peanut and Veal Stew. We've purposely included some of the tried-and-true recipes that were such big hits in *Super Nutrition for Menopause*, like Spring Minestrone, Velvety Borscht, and Asparagus Bisque. They're low in carbohydrates, aromatic, and absolutely flavorful.

Regardless of the season, a good bowl of soup or stew is good any time, anywhere. Since they can be made ahead of time, serving lunch or dinner is a breeze. That can be quite helpful, especially when you've got a heavier-than-usual schedule. Just add one of our nutritiously delicious side salads, and dinner's on the table.

Savory Soups

Getting down to the basics is easy with these three nutritious stock recipes. They're easy to make and loaded with phytonutrients. Make a batch and freeze it for use in future recipes. Or add some heartier vegetables and meat for a scrumptious meal.

VEGETABLE STOCK

Walk through the garden . . . the possibilities are endless.

MAKES ABOUT 2 QUARTS

    4 celery stalks with leaves, cut into 1-inch pieces
    4 carrots, scrubbed and cut into 1-inch pieces
    4 large white onions, chopped
    1 medium turnip, peeled and cut into 1-inch pieces
    6 garlic cloves, crushed
    ½ cup fresh parsley, chopped
    2½ quarts filtered water
       Salt and pepper to taste
    4 fresh thyme sprigs, or 1 teaspoon dried thyme leaves
    2 bay leaves, crumbled

Step 1. Place first six ingredients in a stockpot. Pour in water and season with salt and pepper.

Step 2. Bring liquid to a boil, removing any film that forms on the top.

Step 3. Turn down heat to medium-low and let simmer.

Step 4. Add thyme and crumbled bay leaves.

Step 5. Cover and cook for another hour.

Step 6. Strain the stock into a large bowl, pressing down the juices from the vegetables.

Step 7. Let cool before storing.

BAY LEAVES

From the days of Greek mythology, the noble leaves of the bay laurel tree have certainly held their place in history. This glorious symbol of honor has crowned Olympic champions since 700 B.C. Bay leaf has been used to ease digestive functions and migraines. Applied to the skin, bay leaf oil can help alleviate the symptoms stemming from rheumatism and bruises.

BEEF OR VEAL STOCK

So flavorful, it'll perk up an array of recipes.

MAKES ABOUT 3 QUARTS

3 pounds veal breast, veal shank, or beef shank, cut into 4-inch pieces

3 pounds uncooked veal or beef bones, cracked

3 onions, quartered

3 celery stalks, chopped

3 carrots, peeled and sliced

2 cups water

3 large garlic cloves, pressed

8 black peppercorns

3 quarts filtered water

2 teaspoons fresh thyme, or ½ teaspoon dried thyme leaves

1 bay leaf, crushed

Step 1. Preheat oven to 425°F, then place meat, bones, onion, celery, and carrots in a roasting pan. Roast for 1 hour or until they brown.

Step 2. Transfer the contents of the roasting pan into a 4-quart stockpot.

Step 3. Pour 2 cups water into the roasting pan to incorporate all browned bits of vegetables and meat, then add that to the stockpot.

Step 4. Add garlic and peppercorns to the stockpot, along with 3 quarts water.

Step 5. Bring to a boil; then reduce the temperature to medium-low.

Step 6. Add thyme and bay leaf, and let simmer for 4 hours. (Skim film off the top as necessary.)

Step 7. Strain the stock through a fine strainer.

Step 8. Allow to cool before storing.

CHICKEN OR TURKEY STOCK

How many uses? Let me count the ways . . .

MAKES ABOUT 2½ QUARTS

1 roasting chicken or turkey breast
2½ quarts filtered water
4–5 celery stalks with leaves, chopped
2 large white onions, chopped
1 bay leaf
1 teaspoon fresh basil, chopped
1 teaspoon fresh parsley, chopped
2 large cloves garlic, pressed
½ teaspoon ground cloves
Salt and pepper to taste

Step 1. Place one whole chicken (or turkey breast) in a soup pot and cover with water.

Step 2. Bring to a boil, skimming off fatty froth.

Step 3. Add remaining ingredients, then continue cooking until chicken is done.

Step 4. Remove bay leaf and chicken. Let chicken cool, then debone, saving meat for other recipes.

Step 5. Place breastbone back into soup and let simmer for another 30 to 45 minutes.

Step 6. Remove bone, strain, and let stock cool. Refrigerate or freeze for future use.

HEARTY CHICKEN VEGETABLE SOUP

A soup you can really sink your teeth into!

MAKES 6 SERVINGS

6 cups Chicken Stock (see above)
1½ cups cooked chicken, diced
3 celery stalks with leaves, coarsely chopped
3 carrots, sliced into ½-inch pieces
1 cup rutabaga, coarsely chopped

1 green bell pepper, coarsely chopped
1 cup frozen peas
1 cup mushrooms, chopped
2–3 shallots, coarsely chopped
2 large garlic cloves, pressed
1 teaspoon fresh parsley, chopped
1 teaspoon fresh basil, chopped
1 teaspoon fresh oregano, chopped
½ teaspoon ground cloves
Salt and pepper to taste

Combine ingredients in a soup pot, bring to a boil, then let simmer for at least 1 hour or until vegetables are tender.

MUSHROOM BARLEY SOUP

A classic so delicious, what's not to love?

MAKES 6 SERVINGS

2 ounces dried shiitake mushrooms
¼ cup marsala wine
1 tablespoon high-oleic safflower oil
1 pound crimini mushrooms, cut into ½-inch pieces
2 large carrots, chopped
1 onion, chopped
2 tablespoons flax flour
6 cups Vegetable Stock (page 75)
½ cup pearl barley, rinsed
6 tablespoons slivered, toasted almonds

Step 1. Soak shiitake mushrooms in wine for 20 minutes. Drain. Strain and save wine.

Step 2. Heat oil in a large pot over medium-low heat and add shiitake and crimini mushrooms, carrots, and onions. Cook until onions are translucent.

Step 3. Add flax flour to pot and stir for about 3 to 5 minutes.

Step 4. Blend in wine in which mushrooms soaked and add the Vegetable Stock; bring soup to a boil, stirring frequently.

Step 5. Add barley and lower heat to medium-low and cover.

Step 6. Cook until barley is tender, about 40 minutes.

Step 7. Serve in individual bowls and sprinkle each with 1 tablespoon of slivered almonds.

VEGETABLE MEDLEY SOUP

So delicate . . . it's magnifique!

MAKES 6 SERVINGS

3 celery stalks with leaves, finely chopped
3 carrots, finely chopped
1 large orange or yellow bell pepper, finely chopped
1 cup broccoli, finely chopped
1 cup mushrooms, finely chopped
3 large Vidalia or white onions, finely chopped
1 zucchini, finely diced
6 cups Vegetable Stock (page 75)
5–6 garlic cloves, pressed
1 teaspoon fresh parsley, chopped
1 teaspoon fresh basil, chopped
1 teaspoon fresh marjoram, chopped
Salt and pepper to taste

Step 1. Finely chop veggies (the food processor is easiest), then combine all ingredients in a soup pot.

Step 2. Let simmer for approximately 1 hour or until vegetables are tender.

SPRING MINESTRONE*

Some like it hot, some like it cold. Whichever way it's served, you'll enjoy this celebration of spring.

MAKES 6 SERVINGS

  1 teaspoon high-oleic safflower oil
  1 onion, sliced
1½ quarts filtered water
  2 celery stalks, chopped
  3 medium carrots, cut into rounds
  1 cup broccoli florets
  1 medium potato, cubed
  1 cup mushrooms, sliced
  1 cup green beans, cut into 1-inch pieces
  1 cup sweet peas
  1 teaspoon fresh marjoram, chopped
  1 teaspoon fresh thyme, chopped
  2 tablespoons fresh parsley, chopped
    Salt to taste

Step 1. Lightly oil soup kettle and sauté onion over low heat until translucent.

Step 2. Add water and bring to a boil.

Step 3. Add remaining ingredients, stirring for 1 minute.

Step 4. Cover and let simmer for 20 to 30 minutes.

*CARB ALERT: One serving equals 14 carbohydrate grams.

PARSLEY

A popular garnish for dishes around the globe, this member of the carrot family bursts with vitamins, minerals, and phytoestrogens. It nourishes both kidneys and liver, and gives a wonderful boost to women's health. Rich in chlorophyll, parsley sweetens the breath and aids the digestive process.

GARDEN ROSE SOUP

An absolute favorite around my house!

MAKES 6 SERVINGS

- 9 large garlic cloves, peeled
- 4 tablespoons peanut oil
- 1 tablespoon fresh thyme, chopped
- 1½ quarts Vegetable Stock (page 75)
- ½ teaspoon salt (optional)
- ⅛ teaspoon cayenne
- 2 tablespoons fresh parsley, chopped, for garnish

Step 1. In a soup pot, sauté garlic in oil over low heat for 10 minutes.

Step 2. Add thyme, and continue sautéing over low heat for a few more minutes.

Step 3. Pour off all but 2 tablespoons of the oil; then add Vegetable Stock.

Step 4. Cook over low heat for at least 20 minutes, strain, and discard garlic.

Step 5. Season with salt and cayenne, garnishing with parsley.

LENTIL SOUP*

Naturally nutritious and so good!

MAKES 6 SERVINGS

- 2–3 shallots, chopped
- 3 celery stalks with leaves, chopped
- 4 garlic cloves, chopped
- 1 tablespoon extra-virgin olive oil
- 6 cups Beef Stock or Vegetable Stock (page 76 or 75)
- 1 pound lentils, washed and drained
- 1 medium potato, peeled and diced
- 2 carrots, thinly sliced
- 1 teaspoon fresh basil, chopped
- 1 teaspoon fresh parsley, chopped
- 1 cup tomato sauce
- Salt and pepper to taste

Step 1. Toss shallots, celery, and garlic in pan and sauté in olive oil.

Step 2. Add stock and remaining ingredients, then simmer for at least 1 hour or until vegetables and lentils are done.

*CARB ALERT: One serving equals 19 carbohydrate grams.

QUICK ONION SOUP

A delightful beginning to any meal.

MAKES 6 SERVINGS

3	tablespoons high-oleic sunflower oil
1½	pounds Vidalia onions, thinly sliced
2	tablespoons spelt flour
6	cups Beef Stock (page 76)
	Salt and pepper

Step 1. Place oil in a large pot and heat on medium.

Step 2. Add onions and sauté until brown.

Step 3. Add spelt flour and stir.

Step 4. Gradually mix in stock and simmer for about 30 minutes, stirring and scraping often. Season to taste.

DELICIOUSLY EASY BOUILLABAISSE

Dazzle them with this simple and delicious fish soup.

MAKES 6 SERVINGS

4	tablespoons peanut oil
1	onion, sliced
2	leeks, chopped
1	carrot, chopped
1	celery stalk, chopped
1	pound cod fillet, cut into 2-inch pieces
4	pounds rockfish fillet, cut into 2-inch pieces
2	garlic cloves, chopped
1	bay leaf

1 teaspoon fennel seed
½ cup white wine
2 medium tomatoes, sliced
   Filtered water, as needed
   Salt and pepper to taste
2 tablespoons fresh minced parsley, for garnish

Step 1. Heat oil and sauté onion, leeks, carrot, and celery in a soup pot.

Step 2. Add fish, garlic, bay leaf, and fennel, then sauté a few minutes longer.

Step 3. Add wine, tomatoes, and enough water to cover vegetables and fish.

Step 4. Let simmer for 30 minutes, then season and serve with parsley garnish.

CURRIED CARROT SOUP

A savory twist with a veggie favorite.

MAKES 6 SERVINGS

2 teaspoons extra-virgin olive oil
1 onion, coarsely chopped
5 medium carrots, coarsely chopped
1 teaspoon fresh thyme, chopped
1 tablespoon curry powder
6 cups Chicken Stock or Vegetable Stock (page 77 or 75)
2 tablespoons fresh lemon juice
1½ tablespoons light miso
6 sprigs fresh parsley, for garnish

Step 1. Heat oil in saucepan, gently sautéing onion until translucent.

Step 2. Add carrots and thyme, then stir in curry and sauté for a few more minutes.

Step 3. Add stock and lemon juice, simmering for 30 to 40 minutes.

Step 4. Blend with miso and serve with parsley garnish.

CUCUMBER DILL SOUP*

Having a luncheon? Please your guests with this refreshing soup.

MAKES 6 SERVINGS

6 cucumbers, peeled and cut into 1½-inch-thick slices
4 cups filtered water
3 tablespoons fresh dill, minced
2 tablespoons fresh lemon zest
1 tablespoon light miso
  Juice of 1 lemon
6 sprigs fresh dill, for garnish
6 slices fresh lemon, for garnish

Step 1. Place cucumbers in a soup pot with water, dill, and lemon zest.

Step 2. Cover and let simmer until cucumbers are soft.

Step 3. Purée soup in blender or food processor with miso and lemon juice.

Step 4. Garnish with dill and lemon slices and serve.

*CARB ALERT: One serving equals 10 carbohydrate grams.

THAI PEANUT SOUP

Spicy, delicious—and loaded with omega-9s!

MAKES 4 SERVINGS

1 tablespoon peanut oil
½ cup celery, chopped
2 garlic cloves, minced
4 cups unsalted Chicken Stock (page 77)
2 tablespoons crunchy peanut butter (unsweetened)
1 cup fresh spinach, chopped
  Salt and pepper to taste
4 ounces firm tofu, cubed
2 tablespoons plain yogurt
¼ teaspoon crushed red pepper flakes
2 scallions, chopped, for garnish

Step 1. Heat oil in a large pot on medium, then add celery and garlic.

Step 2. Sauté for about 2 minutes, then pour in Chicken Stock.

Step 3. Add peanut butter and stir to dilute.

Step 4. Bring to a boil, then reduce to a simmer and add spinach.

Step 5. Season with salt and pepper to taste and cook for 15 minutes.

Step 6. Mash tofu and mix with yogurt. Add tofu-yogurt mixture and red pepper flakes to soup.

Step 7. Serve in individual bowls and garnish each with some chopped scallions.

VELVETY BORSCHT*

A colorful and delectable soup.

MAKES 6 SERVINGS

6 large whole beets, peeled
3 large whole carrots, peeled
8 cups filtered water
1½ tablespoons light miso

Step 1. Place beets, carrots, and water in a soup pot, then bring to a boil.

Step 2. Let simmer until vegetables are soft.

Step 3. Remove beets and carrots from water and cut into small pieces.

Step 4. Place vegetables and liquid in a blender or food processor with miso.

Step 5. Blend until smooth, then chill.

*CARB ALERT: One serving equals 17 ¹/₂ carbohydrate grams.

VICHYSSOISE*

An elegant addition to any meal.

MAKES 6 SERVINGS

2 teaspoons high-oleic safflower oil
1 onion, finely chopped
3 leeks, coarsely chopped
2 cups raw steel-cut oats

1   bay leaf
1   sprig fresh thyme
3½ cups Chicken Stock (page 77)
    Salt to taste
1   scallion, chopped, for garnish

Step 1. In heavy saucepan, heat oil and sauté onions and leeks until translucent.

Step 2. Cook oats with bay leaf and thyme in Chicken Stock until soft, about 30 minutes.

Step 3. Discard bay leaf. Purée oats with vegetables in blender or food processor until smooth.

Step 4. Season and garnish with scallions.

*CARB ALERT: One serving equals 13 carbohydrate grams.

ASPARAGUS BISQUE*

Creamy and utterly incredible. Family not keen on asparagus? Try substituting with mushrooms, carrots, broccoli, or spinach.

MAKES 6 SERVINGS

3   cups raw steel-cut oats
12 cups filtered water
3   cups asparagus, cut into ½-inch pieces
4   tablespoons light miso
6   sprigs fresh parsley, for garnish

Step 1. Cook oats in water until soft, about 30 minutes.

Step 2. Add asparagus and cook an additional 10 minutes.

Step 3. Pour soup into blender or food processor with miso and purée.

Step 4. Garnish with parsley and serve.

*CARB ALERT: One serving equals 17 carbohydrate grams.

Stupendous Stews

Warm and soothing, these incredible stews create the perfect mood for family conversation around the dinner table.

VEGETABLE STEW

Wake up your taste buds with this intriguing combination!

MAKES 6 SERVINGS

1 tablespoon peanut oil
1 medium daikon radish, sliced
1 parsnip, diced
3 shiitake mushrooms, soaked in water and sliced
½ cup filtered water
1 tablespoon fresh ginger, grated
1 tablespoon kudzu, diluted in 2 tablespoons cold water
2 tablespoons low-sodium tamari or soy sauce
1 scallion, chopped, for garnish

Step 1. Heat oil in heavy skillet and sauté daikon radish.

Step 2. Add parsnip and shiitake mushrooms, stirring and reducing heat.

Step 3. Add ½ cup water and simmer for 20 minutes.

Step 4. Add ginger and kudzu, then stir until thickened.

Step 5. Season with tamari and garnish with scallion.

MEDITERRANEAN BEEF STEW*

A rich blend of tantalizing tastes.

MAKES 4 TO 6 SERVINGS

1 tablespoon extra-virgin olive oil
2 large green bell peppers, coarsely chopped
1 large onion, coarsely chopped
3 celery stalks with leaves, finely chopped
3–4 garlic cloves, pressed
1 pound stew meat, cut into 1-inch cubes
1 9-ounce package frozen Italian green beans

2 large potatoes, peeled and chopped
1 cup mushrooms, sliced
½ cup fresh parsley, chopped
Filtered water, as needed
1 10¾-ounce can tomato purée
½ cup red wine
1½ teaspoons fresh oregano, chopped
1½ teaspoons fresh basil, chopped
1 bay leaf
1–2 tablespoons agar-agar or arrowroot for thickening, if needed
Salt and pepper to taste

Step 1. Heat olive oil in a large Dutch oven and lightly sauté green peppers, onions, celery, and garlic.

Step 2. Add stew meat and brown on all sides.

Step 3. Add beans, potatoes, mushrooms, parsley, and enough water to cover ingredients.

Step 4. Let cook for approximately 20 minutes, then blend in tomato purée, wine, and remaining seasonings. (Add a little more water throughout cooking process, if needed. However, stew should not be souplike. To thicken, scoop out ¾ cup liquid and thoroughly blend it with agar-agar in a separate bowl, making a smooth, loose paste. Stir back into stew until smooth.)

Step 5. Continue cooking until vegetables and meat are done. Season to taste.

*CARB ALERT: One serving equals 10 to 12 carbohydrate grams.

CHICKEN STEW

A tempting stew with a spicy kick.

MAKES 4 SERVINGS

1 tablespoon extra-virgin olive oil
1 garlic clove, pressed
1 large onion, chopped
4 small chicken breasts, with bones
4 carrots, sliced

1   15-ounce can tomatoes, chopped
1   teaspoon cinnamon
    Pinch of cayenne
1   teaspoon ground cumin
2   tablespoons chunky peanut butter
1½ cups Chicken Broth (page 77)
    Salt and pepper to taste

Step 1. Heat olive oil in a kettle, then sauté garlic and onion until translucent.

Step 2. Add chicken and brown breasts on both sides.

Step 3. Add carrots, tomatoes, cinnamon, cayenne, cumin, and peanut butter. Stir until blended.

Step 4. Add broth and season to taste.

Step 5. Cook over medium-low heat until sauce thickens, about 45 minutes.

VEAL STEW*

An earthy delight from Southern Italy. Terrific over spaghetti squash.

MAKES 4 SERVINGS

1   pound veal stew meat, cut into 1-inch pieces
    Salt and pepper to taste
4   tablespoons extra-virgin olive oil
8   boiling onions, peeled
1   large carrot, chopped
1   celery stalk, chopped
8   medium mushrooms, stemmed
1   tablespoon chopped fresh oregano, or ½ teaspoon dried oregano leaves
1   12-ounce basket cherry tomatoes, stemmed and halved
¼   cup organic marinara sauce

Step 1. Preheat oven to 350°F. Sprinkle veal with salt and pepper.

Step 2. Heat oil in a large pot over medium heat. Add veal, onions, carrot, and celery. Sauté until veal is no longer pink.

Step 3. Mix in mushrooms, oregano, tomatoes, and marinara sauce, then let simmer briefly.

Step 4. Cover pot and transfer to oven. Bake until veal is tender, about 1 hour.

*CARB ALERT: One serving equals 17 carbohydrate grams.

Main-Dish Salads and Dressings

In a hurry? We've got you covered. All of our main-dish salads are quick, nutritious, and sure to please even the most finicky appetite. And when you toss in some seafood and top your salad with one of our omega-rich dressings, your body will thank you.

All you have to do is look at the labels of most grocery store dressings to see that they are loaded with hydrogenated or trans fats. With our easy-to-make alternatives, you get flavor *and* all the health-promoting advantages of the amazing omega-3s. Your family will enjoy each of our ten dressings, especially Lime-Cilantro, Pepita Plum, Templeton's Best, and Orange-Sesame.

For even more dining pleasure, choose one of our delectable soups (featured on pages 74 to 90) to round out your meal. Are you hungry yet? Then get out your chopping board because the fun is about to begin!

Main-Dish Salads

Everything you need is here—colorful phytonutrients, all the omegas, plus plentiful protein ingredients to satisfy the hungriest appetite. Splash on one of our tasty dressings and enjoy.

SUNNY CAESAR SALAD

Did you know that the Caesar salad originated in Mexico? We've crossed the border with this popular classic and gave it an omega boost.

MAKES 4 SERVINGS

1 **head romaine lettuce, chopped**
1 **egg yolk**
2 **garlic cloves**

1 teaspoon Dijon mustard
1 teaspoon Worcestershire sauce
1 tablespoon fresh lemon juice
4 tablespoons extra-virgin olive oil
1 8-ounce can solid white tuna packed in water, drained
1 4-ounce jar sun-dried tomatoes, packed in oil
4 tablespoons Parmesan cheese
4 anchovy fillets, for garnish (optional)
Crushed fresh black pepper

Step 1. Wash, core, and dry lettuce. Tear into ½-inch pieces. Wrap in paper towels, then chill for at least 1 hour.

Step 2. About 10 to 15 minutes before serving, place egg yolk in a large wooden salad bowl. Using the back of a fork, press garlic cloves until a paste is formed.

Step 3. Add mustard, Worcestershire sauce, and lemon juice. Slowly whisk in oil until mixture becomes smooth.

Step 4. Toss together lettuce, dressing, tuna, and sun-dried tomatoes.

Step 5. Sprinkle Parmesan cheese on top. Garnish with anchovy fillets and crushed black pepper, if desired.

TEX-MEX SALAD

A truly unique blend of Southwest cuisine and south-of-the-border ingredients.

MAKES 4 SERVINGS

2 cups red leaf lettuce, finely sliced
1 cup red cabbage, thinly sliced
1 pound cooked chicken breast, chopped
½ red bell pepper, cut julienne
1 cup jicama, cut julienne
1 small avocado, peeled and diced
¼ cup canned black beans, drained and rinsed
¼ red onion, thinly sliced
¼ cup pumpkin seeds

Step 1. Combine all ingredients in a large serving bowl.

Step 2. Coat with a citrus dressing; try the Lime-Cilantro Vinaigrette on page 99.

HAWAIIAN CHICKEN SALAD*

The inviting, sweet scent of pineapple . . . you can almost feel the ocean breeze.

MAKES 6 SERVINGS

1½ pounds cooked chicken breast, cubed or stripped
1 cup scallions, chopped
¾ cup celery, chopped
⅓ cup Spectrum Naturals organic mayonnaise
1 cup pineapple, crushed
1 teaspoon dried tarragon
  Salt and pepper to taste
4 tablespoons extra-virgin olive oil
2 tablespoons apple cider vinegar
2 tablespoons water
6 cups green leaf lettuce, chopped
6 macadamia nuts, chopped

Step 1. Mix chicken, scallions, celery, mayonnaise, pineapple, and tarragon in a large bowl.

Step 2. Season with salt and pepper to taste.

Step 3. In a separate bowl, make vinaigrette by whisking oil, vinegar, and water together.

Step 4. Toss greens and vinaigrette in a large bowl; arrange a single serving on each plate.

Step 5. Top each serving with chicken mixture and a sprinkling of chopped nuts.

*CARB ALERT: One serving equals 12 carbohydrate grams.

HERB-SCENTED CHICKEN SALAD DELUXE*

Takes the ho-hum out of chicken!

MAKES 4 SERVINGS

2	boneless chicken breasts, cut into strips
2–3	tablespoons white wine
1	tablespoon extra-virgin olive oil
4	garlic cloves, pressed
1	teaspoon fresh oregano, chopped
1	teaspoon fresh basil, chopped
1	teaspoon fresh marjoram, chopped
	Salt and pepper
1–1½	large bunches red leaf lettuce, gently torn into small pieces
2–3	tomatoes, sliced
⅓	cup carrot, coarsely grated
1	large green bell pepper, chopped
1	yellow or orange bell pepper, chopped
3	celery stalks, chopped
1	white onion, chopped
¾	cup mushrooms, chopped
⅓	cup black olives, chopped
1	avocado, sliced
7½	ounces garbanzo beans or chickpeas (½ can)
¼	cup walnuts, chopped

Step 1. Marinate cut-up chicken breasts in wine and set in refrigerator, either while chopping other ingredients or overnight.

Step 2. Pour olive oil into skillet and warm, then toss in garlic.

Step 3. Turn up heat and add chicken breasts; brown on all sides. Reduce heat and sprinkle chicken with seasonings. Cook until done.

Step 4. Meanwhile, place lettuce and remaining ingredients into a large salad bowl and toss.

Step 5. Coat salad with your choice of our dressings.

Step 6. Top with cooked chicken strips and serve.

*CARB ALERT: One serving equals 17 carbohydrate grams.

CALIFORNIA SALMON SALAD*

*The delectable flavor of salmon blends beautifully with the
sweet-sour taste of balsamic vinegar.*

MAKES 4 SERVINGS

8 tablespoons extra-virgin olive oil
4 tablespoons balsamic vinegar
  Salt and pepper to taste
¼ cup Vegetable Stock (page 75) or fish broth
4 salmon fillets, 4 ounces each
6 cups baby greens
2 tablespoons capers, drained
½ small red onion, thinly sliced
4 tablespoons cooked corn kernels

Step 1. Whisk 6 tablespoons oil and 3 tablespoons vinegar in a small
bowl. Season with salt and pepper and set aside.

Step 2. In a large sauté pan, add the remaining tablespoon of vinegar,
2 tablespoons oil, and the broth. Heat to a boil, then reduce
temperature and add the salmon.

Step 3. Poach for about 15 to 20 minutes, then transfer to a plate and
allow to cool.

Step 4. Prepare each serving plate with 1½ cups baby greens. Add
salmon fillet and garnish with capers, red onion, and corn.

Step 5. Drizzle balsamic vinaigrette over each serving.

*CARB ALERT: One serving equals 11 carbohydrate grams.

PEANUTS

Peanuts take center stage in many West African dishes,
from soups to stews. And a delightful peanut sauce is
frequently used in Indonesian and Malaysian recipes.

MANGO SALMON SALAD*

A tantalizing, tropical combo.

MAKES 4 SERVINGS

- 1 15-ounce can salmon, flaked
- ½ teaspoon oregano
- 1 large garlic clove, pressed
- ¼ teaspoon fresh dill, chopped
- Salt and pepper to taste
- 1–1½ large heads red leaf lettuce, gently torn into small pieces
- ½ small basket cherry tomatoes
- 3 scallions, chopped
- ⅓ cup carrot, coarsely grated
- 2 orange or yellow bell peppers, chopped
- 2 celery stalks, chopped
- 1 cucumber, chopped
- ½ cup alfalfa sprouts (optional)
- ½ cup peanuts
- 2 large mangoes, peeled and chopped

Step 1. Blend salmon with spices and set aside.

Step 2. Place lettuce and remaining ingredients (except salmon and mango) into a large salad bowl and toss.

Step 3. Dress salad with one of our delicious dressings, such as Balsamic-Hazelnut (featured on page 101).

Step 4. Toss in salmon and mango, lightly blend, and serve.

*CARB ALERT: One serving equals 17 carbohydrate grams.

OLIVE-TUNA SALAD

An omega-rich treasure as easy as one-two-three!

MAKES 4 SERVINGS

- ¼ cup extra-virgin olive oil
- ¼ cup balsamic vinegar
- 1 small red onion, thinly sliced

16 ounces solid white tuna packed in water, drained and separated into chunks

¼ cup black olives, sliced

¼ cup fresh parsley, chopped

Salt and pepper to taste

6 cups romaine lettuce, chopped

⅓ cup slivered almonds, toasted, for garnish

Step 1. In a large bowl, whisk oil and vinegar together.

Step 2. Blend in onion, tuna, olives, and parsley. Season with salt and pepper.

Step 3. Place 1½ cups of lettuce on each serving plate.

Step 4. Top each plate with tuna mixture. Garnish with almonds.

STARBURST TUNA SALAD*

A pretty—and totally scrumptious—salad that's easy to prepare.

MAKES 4 SERVINGS

16 ounces solid white tuna packed in water, drained and separated into chunks

4 large garlic cloves, pressed

2 teaspoons fresh oregano, chopped

1½ teaspoons ground cumin

1 teaspoon fresh basil, chopped

1 teaspoon fresh parsley, chopped

Salt and pepper to taste

½ teaspoon Dijon mustard

2 shallots, finely chopped

4 lettuce leaves or 16 spinach leaves, stemmed

4 radishes, flowered

2 large avocados, peeled and sliced into quarters lengthwise

2 cucumbers, peeled and sliced into ¼-inch pieces

2 papayas, peeled and quartered

2 tomatoes, quartered

Step 1. Put drained tuna chunks, herbs, and seasonings into a bowl and blend well.

Step 2. Stir in mustard and chopped shallots.

Step 3. Place lettuce or spinach leaves in the center of a serving plate. Top with four individual scoops of herbed tuna, placing a flowered radish in the center of each scoop.

Step 4. Arrange avocado slices opposite each other around each tuna scoop.

Step 5. Fill in avocado gaps by alternating 2 to 3 cucumber slices with papaya and tomato slices. Have family or guests serve themselves.

*CARB ALERT: One serving equals 20 carbohydrate grams.

SOUTH SEA CRAB SALAD*

A tasty kaleidoscope of colors—packed with omega-3s and omega-9s.

MAKES 4 SERVINGS

  1 pound white crabmeat, fresh or canned
  1 small papaya, cubed
  1 California avocado, cubed
  ½ honeydew melon, cubed
  4 cups greens
 12 macadamia nuts
  4 mint sprigs, for garnish
     Citrus-Twister Dressing (page 103)

Step 1. Place the crabmeat in a bowl and flake with a fork.

Step 2. Combine papaya, avocado, and melon in a bowl, then stir in crabmeat.

Step 3. Arrange 1 cup of greens on four individual plates. Top with fruit-and-crab mixture.

Step 4. Sprinkle nuts over each serving.

Step 5. Spoon Citrus-Twister Dressing over each serving; then garnish with mint sprigs.

HEALTHY FUN TWIST: Try canned shrimp instead of crabmeat.

*CARB ALERT: One serving equals 16 carbohydrate grams.

BASIL-GARLIC SEAFOOD SALAD*

Got a hungry bunch? Problem solved with this hearty main-event salad!

MAKES 4 SERVINGS

1 pound seafood, such as bay shrimp, scallops, lobster, or crabmeat (your choice)
1 large head romaine lettuce, gently torn into small pieces
2 large tomatoes, chopped
1 large green bell pepper, chopped
2 celery stalks, chopped
1 carrot, chopped
1 large Vidalia onion, chopped
1 cucumber, peeled and chopped
1 avocado, peeled and sliced
1 cup broccoli florets, chopped
½ cup green olives with pimientos, chopped
½ cup alfalfa sprouts
4 large garlic cloves, minced
2 teaspoons fresh basil, chopped
1 teaspoon fresh oregano, chopped
1 teaspoon fresh marjoram, chopped
Salt and pepper to taste
½ lemon
2 tablespoons virgin or extra-virgin olive oil

Step 1. Place first twelve ingredients into a large salad bowl and toss.

Step 2. Sprinkle in herbs and seasonings, and squeeze lemon over salad. Lightly toss.

Step 3. Drizzle oil over salad, again tossing lightly, and serve.

*CARB ALERT: One serving equals 19 carbohydrate grams.

Delectable Dressings

Looking for a quick way to add healthy omega oils to family meals? Look no further. Just splash one of our incredibly delicious dressings on a salad. With such an intriguing variety, you'll enjoy a gamut of taste sensations. And when you make them with fresh herbs, they're even better. Refrigerate any leftover salad dressings.

LIME-CILANTRO VINAIGRETTE

Give your taste buds a wake-up call with this citrus dressing. It's especially good on our Tex-Mex Salad, featured on page 91.

MAKES ¼ CUP

- ⅓ cup green onions, chopped
- 2 tablespoons fresh lime juice
- 2 tablespoons fresh cilantro, chopped
- 1 tablespoon honey mustard
- 2 tablespoons walnut oil
  Salt and pepper to taste

Step 1. Combine first four ingredients in a medium bowl.

Step 2. Gradually whisk in walnut oil, then season with salt and pepper to taste.

TEMPLETON'S BEST DRESSING

An absolute favorite in our home—we just know you'll love it, too, courtesy of James William Templeton.

MAKES ¾ CUP

- 1 kiwi fruit, peeled and chopped
- ¼ cup fresh lime juice
- ½ cup filtered water
- 2 tablespoons tahini
- 1 teaspoon maple syrup
  Sea salt to taste
- ⅓ cup pumpkin seeds, toasted

Step 1. In blender, add first six ingredients in order and blend.

Step 2. Be sure to add pumpkin seeds last to give crunch to dressing.

PEPITA PLUM DRESSING

This five-star dressing gets a standing ovation every time, whether you use it on a salad or as a dip for your favorite veggies.

MAKES 1 CUP

1 cup pumpkin seeds
1 cup filtered water
2–3 umeboshi plums, to taste
2 tablespoons flax oil

Step 1. Wash and dry pumpkin seeds, then dry roast them in a skillet over medium heat until they puff up and pop.

Step 2. Place roasted seeds in blender and grind to meal-like consistency.

Step 3. Add water to blender and continue mixing. Add plums and oil, blending until desired taste is reached. (The more plums you add, the saltier the dressing.)

FRENCH RIVIERA DRESSING

Great as a dressing or for flavoring a sauté.

MAKES ⅓ CUP

⅓ cup extra-virgin olive oil
3 tablespoons fresh lemon juice
2 garlic cloves, pressed
1 teaspoon fresh tarragon, chopped
1 teaspoon Dijon mustard
   Salt and freshly ground pepper to taste

Put ingredients in a small covered jar and shake vigorously for 30 seconds.

LEMON-SCENTED DRESSING

A delicate taste that's a delightful accent to any fish meal.

MAKES ⅓ CUP

⅓ cup light sesame oil
3 tablespoons fresh lemon juice
1 tablespoon fresh lemon zest
½ teaspoon fresh basil, chopped
½ teaspoon fresh rosemary, chopped
  Salt to taste

Put ingredients in a small covered jar and shake vigorously for 30 seconds.

BALSAMIC-HAZELNUT DRESSING

Remarkable—and absolutely unforgettable.

MAKES ⅓ CUP

⅓ cup hazelnut oil
2 tablespoons balsamic vinegar or apple cider vinegar
1 large garlic clove, minced
½ teaspoon fresh savory, chopped
  Salt and pepper to taste

Put ingredients in a small covered jar and shake vigorously for 30 seconds.

GINGERY GARLIC DRESSING

An intriguing spice combo that zings! Also great for sautéing.

MAKES ⅓ CUP

⅓ cup peanut oil
1½ tablespoons fresh ginger, finely chopped
1 tablespoon fresh basil, chopped
8 large garlic cloves, minced
  Salt and freshly ground pepper to taste

Put ingredients in a small covered jar and shake vigorously for 30 seconds.

PAPAYA DRESSING

A sweet delight, this light summery dressing is especially good on wild or mixed greens.

MAKES ⅓ CUP

⅓ cup high-oleic safflower oil
1 tablespoon papaya juice concentrate
2 teaspoons finely chopped Vidalia onion
½ teaspoon fresh thyme, chopped
½ teaspoon fresh marjoram, chopped
Salt to taste

Put ingredients in a small covered jar and shake vigorously for 30 seconds.

ORANGE-SESAME DRESSING

A wondrous twist you've just gotta try.

MAKES ½ CUP

¼ cup fresh orange juice
2 tablespoons apple cider vinegar
¼ cup extra-virgin olive oil
1 teaspoon sesame seed oil
Salt and pepper to taste
6 teaspoons sesame seeds, for topping

Step 1. Whisk orange juice, vinegar, and oils together.

Step 2. Season with salt and pepper to taste.

Step 3. Drizzle over salad and sprinkle each serving with approximately 1 teaspoon of sesame seeds.

CITRUS-TWISTER DRESSING

An excellent choice for South Sea Crab Salad (see page 97).

MAKES ½ CUP

- ¼ cup walnut oil
- 2 tablespoons fresh lime juice
- 1 teaspoon fresh lemon zest
- 1 tablespoons honey mustard
- Salt and pepper to taste

Step 1. Whisk oil and juice together.

Step 2. Stir in lemon zest and honey mustard.

Step 3. Season to taste.

Vibrant Vegetables

What's the trick in turning any meal into a memorable event? Serve spectacular side dishes . . . we have plenty of choices for you.

Whether served as a side salad or a delightful companion to an entrée, each of our recipes will help fortify your family's health. They're loaded with fiber and colorful pigments, which give them their antioxidant power to halt disease in its tracks. In fact, there are over five thousand antioxidants found in plant foods. Many plant foods contain specific health-enhancing phytonutrients, such as sulforaphane (broccoli), flavonoids (citrus fruits, carrots, cabbage, and tomatoes), and sulfides (onions and garlic).

Consequently, adding these wonderful ingredients isn't just for taste appeal, but for health appeal as well. So have fun and paint your plates with a rainbow of healthy colors, choosing from broccoli, carrots, brussels sprouts, cabbage, kale, beans, eggplant, peppers, and so many delicious others. These tasty side dishes are also a terrific way to get your kids running to the dinner table for those all-too-important omega-rich foods they need for their developing brains. A vegetable emphasis will also translate into a shrinking waistline!

Be sure to check out the yummy Jicama Slaw, Gingersnap Squash, Spicy Eggplant, and Minty Mashed Cauliflower recipes. Vegetables never tasted so good!

On-the-Side Salads

These veggie combos are so delectable, they just might steal the show. Dressed up with some dazzling omega oils, your meals will get the healthy boost they need.

BRUSSELS SPROUTS TWIST

Refreshing with a flavorful bite.

MAKES 4 SERVINGS

1 pound brussels sprouts, ends trimmed
2 tablespoons fresh lemon juice
2 teaspoons Dijon mustard
¼ cup extra-virgin olive oil
1 teaspoon fresh thyme, chopped
   Salt and pepper to taste
4 tablespoons walnuts, toasted and chopped

Step 1. Steam sprouts until tender (about 8 minutes); then drain.

Step 2. Meanwhile, make dressing: Combine lemon juice, mustard, oil, and thyme in a bowl and season to taste.

Step 3. Place dressing in a large skillet and heat.

Step 4. Add sprouts and lightly toss until warm.

Step 5. Sprinkle each serving with 1 tablespoon chopped walnuts.

NUTTY BROCCOLI-CAULIFLOWER SALAD*

One zesty medley.

MAKES 6 SERVINGS

6 cups broccoli florets
6 cups cauliflower florets
2 teaspoons low-sodium soy sauce
2 tablespoons rice vinegar
2 teaspoons sesame seed oil

¼ cup extra-virgin olive oil
1 tablespoon fresh ginger, grated
1 garlic clove, pressed
6 tablespoons pecans, chopped and toasted

Step 1. Steam broccoli and cauliflower until tender-crisp, about 5 minutes.

Step 2. Transfer vegetables to a large bowl and let cool.

Step 3. Whisk soy sauce, rice vinegar, sesame seed oil, and olive oil in a small bowl; then stir in ginger and garlic.

Step 4. Pour over broccoli-cauliflower mixture, and let marinate until serving time.

Step 5. Sprinkle each serving with 1 tablespoon toasted pecans.

HELPFUL TIP: Put chopped pecans in a heavy skillet. Toast over medium heat for approximately 5 minutes. Let cool.

*CARB ALERT: One serving equals 12 carbohydrate grams.

FIELD OF GREENS

Just make it—and they'll enjoy.

MAKES 2 TO 4 SERVINGS

2 cups mixed field greens or salad greens (your choice)
½ cup broccoli florets, finely chopped
2 red radishes, sliced
¼ cup black olives, minced
½ cup sprouts
Salt to taste
Sunflower seeds, toasted

Toss ingredients together and drizzle with one of the omega-rich dressings featured on pages 99 to 103.

SAUCY RED CABBAGE*

A sweet-and-sour delectable treat from Italy.

MAKES 4 SERVINGS

- 4 tablespoons sesame oil
- 1 teaspoon anise seeds, toasted
- 1 red onion, thinly sliced
- 1½ pounds red cabbage, thinly sliced
- ¼ cup fresh orange juice
- 2 tablespoons dried cranberries
- ½ cup balsamic vinegar

Step 1. Heat oil in a large skillet over medium heat. Add anise seeds and toast for 1 minute or less.

Step 2. Stir in onion and sauté until translucent.

Step 3. Add cabbage and cook until wilted, about 5 minutes.

Step 4. Pour in orange juice, then stir in cranberries and vinegar.

Step 5. Cook over medium-high heat until juice reduces.

Step 6. Lower heat and simmer for 20 minutes. Stir often to prevent caramelizing. Serve immediately.

*CARB ALERT: One serving equals 14 carbohydrate grams.

ARTICHOKE JUMBLE

This recipe combines Mediterranean favorites in one crowd-winning mix.

MAKES 4 SERVINGS

- ¼ cup extra-virgin olive oil
- 3 tablespoons fresh basil, chopped
- 2 tablespoons balsamic vinegar
- 1 pound roma tomatoes, chopped
- 1 14-ounce can artichoke hearts, drained
- 1 small red onion, chopped
- 8 black olives, chopped
  Salt and pepper to taste
- 4 teaspoons feta cheese, for garnish

Step 1. Whisk oil, basil, and vinegar in a medium bowl.

Step 2. Add tomatoes, artichoke hearts, red onion, and olives and toss to blend.

Step 3. Season with salt and pepper to taste.

Step 4. Sprinkle each serving with 1 teaspoon feta cheese.

JICAMA SLAW

This slaw's got real personality! Jicama, a Mexican potato, is sweet, crunchy, and full of fiber.

MAKES 4 SERVINGS

12 ounces jicama, peeled and cut julienne
 1 large red bell pepper, cut julienne
 1 yellow bell pepper, cut julienne
 2 tablespoons fresh lime juice
 1 tablespoon Spectrum Naturals organic mayonnaise
 1 garlic clove, pressed
 1 teaspoon fresh ginger, shredded
 1 teaspoon chili powder
    Salt and pepper to taste
 ¼ cup fresh cilantro, finely chopped
 4 tablespoons pumpkin seeds, toasted for garnish

Step 1. Combine jicama and peppers in a bowl, then set aside.

Step 2. Purée lime juice, mayonnaise, garlic, ginger, and chili powder in a blender. Season to taste with salt and pepper.

Step 3. Pour blended dressing over jicama-pepper mix, add cilantro, and lightly stir until coated.

Step 4. Sprinkle pumpkin seeds on top.

SICILIAN BLISS

Packed with tomato power—and a snap to make. Whatever the entrée, from meat to seafood, this easy side salad makes a tasty companion.

MAKES 4 SERVINGS

2 large tomatoes, sliced
⅓ cup onions or scallions, chopped
1 tablespoon extra-virgin olive oil
½ tablespoon red wine vinegar
1 teaspoon fresh oregano, chopped
1 teaspoon fresh basil, chopped
   Salt and pepper to taste
   Parsley sprigs, for garnish (optional)

Step 1. Arrange sliced tomatoes on a serving plate and top with onions.

Step 2. Pour oil and vinegar evenly over ingredients.

Step 3. Sprinkle on seasonings; garnish with parsley, if desired.

On-the-Side Veggies

These versatile vegetables—bursting with phytonutrients and color—offer a whole new repertoire of savory sides that are the perfect accompaniment to any meal.

ZIPPY GREEN MIX

Tangy and delicious. Try bok choy, broccoli, cabbage, collards, dandelion greens, escarole, mustard greens, spinach, Swiss chard, turnip greens, or watercress.

MAKES 4 SERVINGS

2 pounds greens, trimmed and cleaned
   Filtered water, as needed
2 tablespoons extra-virgin olive oil
1 garlic clove, minced
   Pinch of sea salt
   Red pepper flakes (optional)
1 tablespoon almonds, sliced, for topping

Step 1. Place greens in a pot and add just enough water to cover. Simmer until greens are barely tender, approximately 4 to 7 minutes.

Step 2. Drain greens, then chop coarsely and set aside.

Step 3. Heat olive oil in 2-quart saucepan and sauté garlic over low heat until it turns pale golden brown.

Step 4. Turn off heat and quickly add greens. Add sea salt to taste and sprinkle on hot pepper flakes, if desired.

Step 5. Set over low heat, cooking gently by turning greens several times. Trickle in some water as needed to prevent scorching, and cook until tender. (Do not overcook; depending on the greens used, they may not need further cooking.)

Step 6. Serve with sliced almonds sprinkled on top.

BROCCOLI CRUNCH

A dish that plays well with others—try it with almost anything!
It adds powerful nutrients to your meal.

MAKES 4 SERVINGS

1 head broccoli, stems and florets, chopped
¼ cup hazelnut oil or extra-virgin olive oil
⅔ cup shallots, chopped
1 teaspoon fresh rosemary, chopped
  Salt and pepper to taste
¼ cup hazelnuts, toasted and chopped

Step 1. Steam broccoli in a large pot until tender (about 5 minutes), then drain and set aside.

Step 2. In a large skillet, heat oil, then sauté shallots until tender, about 3 minutes.

Step 3. Add rosemary and broccoli, toss until heated through, and season to taste.

Step 4. Add chopped hazelnuts and toss. Serve.

VEGGIE SAUTÉ*

A zippy fusion of flavors.

MAKES 4 SERVINGS

     1 head broccoli, cut into florets
    18 okra, fresh or frozen
     1 tablespoon extra-virgin olive oil
   2–3 garlic cloves, minced (optional)
     1 6-ounce jar marinated artichoke hearts, drained and halved
        Pinch of red pepper flakes
        Juice of 1 lime

Step 1. Steam broccoli florets until tender-crisp, then plunge into cold water.

Step 2. Quickly boil okra, remove from pan, and let cool.

Step 3. Heat skillet on medium, add oil, and stir in garlic if desired.

Step 4. Add artichoke hearts; cook 3 minutes.

Step 5. Add broccoli and okra with a pinch of red pepper flakes to the skillet and stir.

Step 6. Remove from heat and stir in lime juice.

*CARB ALERT: One serving equals 16 carbohydrate grams.

GRILLED ASPARAGUS

It's summertime and the living is . . . delicious! But don't let inclement weather stop you . . . get creative and use your broiler or inside grill.

MAKES 4 SERVINGS

     2 tablespoons extra-virgin olive oil
     1 pound fresh asparagus, trimmed
     4 tablespoons walnuts, toasted
        Salt and pepper to taste

Step 1. Prepare barbecue or inside grill.

Step 2. Drizzle oil over asparagus and grill until tender, about 5 minutes.

Step 3. Meanwhile, heat a small skillet and add walnuts, toasting and tossing for 2 minutes.

Step 4. Transfer asparagus to platter and season to taste.

Step 5. Top with walnuts and enjoy warm or at room temperature.

ROASTED SUMMER DELIGHT*

Incredibly easy . . . undeniably delicious! Other favorite grilling vegetables are portobello mushrooms, leeks, corn, and eggplant. The longer you marinate them, the moister and more flavorful they'll be.

MAKES 4 SERVINGS

1 tablespoon fresh lemon juice
1 tablespoon balsamic vinegar
2 teaspoons prepared stone-ground mustard
3 tablespoons extra-virgin olive oil
Pinch of sea salt
4–5 fresh basil leaves, finely minced, or
1 tablespoon fresh dill, finely minced
1 large red onion, quartered
2 medium zucchini, thickly sliced
2 yellow summer squash, thickly sliced
4 medium tomatoes

Step 1. Whisk first six ingredients together for marinade.

Step 2. Place vegetables in shallow glass baking dish and pour marinade over them.

Step 3. Refrigerate and marinate for about 30 minutes.

Step 4. Meanwhile, preheat grill and lightly oil rack.

Step 5. Arrange vegetable slices on rack. Grill and baste with leftover marinade, turning as needed.

*CARB ALERT: One serving equals 17 carbohydrate grams.

MINT

In Caesar's times, this refreshing herb symbolized hospitality. Its soothing and cooling properties help upset stomachs, digestive problems, and menstrual cramps. With its antioxidant and antiviral power, mint has also been used for bronchitis, colds, coughs, sore throats, and infections.

GREEN BEAN–SQUASH DUO*

A dish for all seasons!

MAKES 4 SERVINGS

1   cup butternut squash, peeled and cubed
1   pound green beans, snapped and veined
2   tablespoons extra-virgin olive oil
1   garlic clove, minced
½   cup Chicken Stock (page 77)
    Salt and pepper to taste
¼   cup pine nuts, toasted
¼   cup fresh mint, chopped

Step 1. Place squash in a large pot of boiling water. Cook for 15 to 20 minutes or until soft. Drain and set aside.

Step 2. Meanwhile, place green beans in a large skillet filled with 2 inches of water. Simmer for 5 to 10 minutes until crisp.

Step 3. Remove and set aside.

Step 4. In the same skillet, heat oil and add garlic; sauté for 1 minute.

Step 5. Stir in string beans and toss to coat, then add squash and Chicken Stock. Heat until warm.

Step 6. Season to taste and place veggies in a large serving bowl.

Step 7. Blend pine nuts and mint with vegetables. Serve warm.

*CARB ALERT: One serving equals 14 carbohydrate grams.

GOLDEN TARRAGON SQUASH*

Blessed with a buttery taste, this tasty dish is packed with vitamin A.

MAKES 4 SERVINGS

> 2 acorn squash (3 pounds total), peeled and cut into
> ½-inch cubes
> ½ cup almond milk
> ¼ teaspoon cayenne
> Salt and pepper to taste
> ½ cup fresh tarragon, chopped
> ½ cup pepitas or pumpkin seeds, toasted

Step 1. Cook squash in boiling water until soft, about 20 minutes.

Step 2. Drain water and add almond milk; simmer.

Step 3. Add cayenne pepper, then season to taste.

Step 4. Place in a serving bowl and add tarragon and pepitas. Serve warm.

*CARB ALERT: One serving equals 16 carbohydrate grams.

GINGERSNAP SQUASH

Delicate sweet-and-sour aromas dance with the smooth taste of avocado.

MAKES 6 SERVINGS

> 7 cups Vegetable Stock (page 75)
> 1 stalk lemon grass, halved
> 1 1-inch piece ginger, peeled and slivered
> ½ cinnamon stick
> ½ teaspoon cayenne pepper
> 2 medium zucchini, peeled and quartered lengthwise,
> then thinly sliced
> 1 pound firm tofu, cut into 1-inch cubes
> ¼ cup fresh lemon juice
> ¾ cup fresh cilantro, chopped
> 1 small avocado, cubed, for garnish

Step 1. Combine first five ingredients in a large pot and bring to a boil.

Step 2. Reduce heat and simmer for 10 minutes.

Step 3. Strain broth and return back to pot, discarding any solids.

Step 4. Bring liquid to a boil and add zucchini and tofu. Reduce heat and cook for about 7 minutes.

Step 5. Stir in lemon juice and cilantro; top each serving with cubed avocado.

SPAGHETTI SQUASH TOSS

Can something this fun be this easy and nutritious? You bet. And it's a great stand-in for higher-carbohydrate pasta.

MAKES 4 SERVINGS

    1   spaghetti squash
        Salt and pepper to taste
    2   large garlic cloves, pressed
    ½   teaspoon cinnamon
  1–2   tablespoons extra-virgin olive oil

Step 1. Place squash in a large pot and cover with water. Boil until tender, about 30 minutes; let cool. Cut squash in half.

Step 2. With a fork, separate (unthread) the spaghetti pulp from the skin and place in serving dish.

Step 3. Sprinkle on seasonings and oil, tossing lightly.

GREEN AND YELLOW STIR-FRY

A quick and easy dish with a lot of eye appeal.

MAKES 4–5 SERVINGS

    3   medium green zucchini, trimmed
    2   medium yellow zucchini, trimmed
    3   tablespoons extra-virgin olive oil
        Salt and pepper to taste
    2   garlic cloves, peeled and finely minced
    6   large basil leaves, cut into thin strips

Step 1. Cut zucchini lengthwise and scoop out seedy center. Cut into ¼-inch slices.

Step 2. Heat a heavy skillet and add oil. Toss in zucchini with salt and pepper, and sauté for 2 minutes.

Step 3. Reduce heat and add garlic and basil; cook for 1 minute. (Zucchini should be crisp.)

VEGETABLE LATKES*

An omega twist to an old-world favorite!

MAKES 4 SERVINGS (1 SERVING = 3 LATKES)

½ **pound carrots, peeled**
1 **pound butternut squash**
½ **pound parsnips**
¼ **cup flax flour**
¼ **cup fresh dill, chopped**
¼ **cup green onions, chopped**
   Salt and pepper to taste
2 **large eggs, beaten**
3 **tablespoons extra-virgin olive oil (more as needed)**

Step 1. Shred peeled carrots, squash, and parsnips in a food processor. Squeeze out excess moisture with paper towels.

Step 2. Blend flour, dill, onions, salt, and pepper in a large bowl.

Step 3. Add shredded vegetables and toss to coat.

Step 4. Blend in eggs.

Step 5. Heat oil in a large skillet over medium heat.

Step 6. Using a large soup spoon, shape vegetable mix into 4-inch rounds. Cook until brown, flipping once. Repeat with remaining batter. Add more oil as needed.

Step 7. Accompany with a dollop of applesauce, sour cream, or plain yogurt. Serve hot.

*CARB ALERT: One serving equals 12 carbohydrate grams.

ESCAROLE MIX*

A great companion to Italian meals.

MAKES 4 SERVINGS

4 tablespoons extra-virgin olive oil
2 garlic cloves, pressed
1 small red onion, thinly sliced
1 head escarole, trimmed and rinsed
½ cup fresh basil, chopped
4 roma tomatoes, seeded and chopped
1 15-ounce can cannellini beans, rinsed and drained
Salt and pepper to taste

Step 1. Heat 1 tablespoon oil in skillet and sauté garlic and onion about 2 minutes.

Step 2. Add half the escarole and cook until wilted. Transfer to a serving bowl.

Step 3. Sauté remaining escarole, adding oil if needed. Add to bowl.

Step 4. Heat remaining oil and sauté basil, tomatoes, and cannellini beans until warm, about 5 minutes. Season to taste. Mix with escarole.

*CARB ALERT: Each serving equals 12 carbohydrate grams.

SPICY EGGPLANT

A robust sensation!

MAKES 4 SERVINGS

4 Chinese or Asian eggplants, or 1 regular eggplant (about 1 pound)
Salt
½ cup fresh basil, chopped
¼ cup Chicken Stock (page 77)
2 green onions, chopped
1 large garlic clove, minced
1 tablespoon fresh ginger, grated
¼ teaspoon crushed red pepper flakes
4 tablespoons walnut oil
Sesame seeds, for garnish

Step 1. Cut Chinese eggplants in half lengthwise. (Cut regular eggplant lengthwise into ¼-inch-wide slices, then cut crosswise.)

Step 2. Salt eggplant and allow to stand for 20 minutes. Pat dry.

Step 3. Place basil, stock, onions, garlic, ginger, and red pepper flakes into a blender and blend until combined.

Step 4. Heat oil in a large skillet and cook eggplant until tender, about 5 minutes, turning once. Remove and set aside.

Step 5. Add basil mixture to skillet and warm.

Step 6. Return eggplant to skillet and heat until warmed through.

Step 7. Sprinkle eggplant with sesame seeds and serve immediately.

WARM CAULIFLOWER SALAD

Short on prep time, long on flavor.

MAKES 4 SERVINGS

1 head cauliflower, florets separated
1–2 tablespoons flax oil
Salt and pepper to taste
1 teaspoon fresh parsley or chives, chopped

Step 1. Add cauliflower to a pot of boiling water and cook until crisp, about 5 minutes.

Step 2. Remove with slotted spoon and place on serving plate.

Step 3. Drizzle with flax oil and sprinkle with salt and pepper and parsley or chives. Serve warm.

MINTY MASHED CAULIFLOWER

Who needs starchy mashed potatoes?
Here's a scrumptious alternative your family will enjoy.

MAKES 4 SERVINGS

1 head cauliflower, cut up
¼ cup Chicken Stock (page 77)
4 tablespoons extra-virgin olive oil
¼ cup fresh mint, chopped
Salt and pepper to taste

Step 1. Place cauliflower in a large pot and add water to top; bring to a boil.

Step 2. When water begins to boil, lower to a simmer and cover.

Step 3. Cook for about 15 minutes. Drain, place back in pot, and mash.

Step 4. Blend in stock, oil, and mint. Season to taste. Serve hot.

Succulent Seafood

What lurks beneath the sea? Omega-rich treasures galore! Eating two or more seafood meals a week can do a great deal to boost your omega-3 levels as well as slim your figure. And that translates to better health. The fattier fish (good fat, that is) are salmon, tuna, herring, anchovies, trout, mackerel, and whitefish. But don't dismiss their other compadres, such as shrimp, halibut, cod, flounder, crab, catfish, or snapper. They all do their part in the bigger equation of helping you and your family enjoy a healthier, more nutritious lifestyle.

Without much fuss, you can serve your family or friends nutritiously delicious meals such as Snapper Crunch, Salmon and Eggplant Tango, Crab Cake Casserole, Coco-Nutty Shrimp, and Outrageous Tuna Burgers. Just complete the meal with a salad or one of our simple side veggies, then watch everyone munch away with delight.

CITRUS-RAINBOW TROUT*

The secret? It's in the sauce! This recipe also works well with other omega-3 fish such as salmon.

MAKES 4 SERVINGS

1 medium orange (also use peel)
1 lemon (also use peel)
½ pink grapefruit
½ cup fresh mint, chopped
4 tablespoons extra-virgin olive oil
1 cup red onion, chopped

4 tablespoons apple cider vinegar
4 tablespoons yellow cornmeal
2 tablespoons flax flour
2 trout (1½ pounds each), boned and cut in half
   Salt and pepper to taste
2 tablespoons macadamia nuts, chopped
1 tablespoon fresh chives, chopped, for garnish

Step 1. Grate 1 teaspoon orange peel and 1 teaspoon lemon peel. Peel orange and grapefruit and cut into ½-inch pieces. Cut lemon into eight pieces.

Step 2. Mix fruit pieces with mint in a small bowl.

Step 3. Heat 1 tablespoon oil in a large pan over medium heat. Add onion and cook until translucent. Pour in vinegar and cook for 2 to 3 minutes, then add to fruit mix.

Step 4. Blend cornmeal and flax flour in a separate bowl.

Step 5. Sprinkle trout with salt and pepper, then dip into flour mixture, coating both sides.

Step 6. Add remaining oil to the same skillet and sauté fish until crisp. Turn and let cook until center of fish is opaque.

Step 7. Top with fruit relish, and sprinkle with macadamia nuts. Garnish with chives.

*CARB ALERT: One serving equals 15 carbohydrate grams.

DILL

Anglo-Saxons used this herb from the parsley family to ease digestive disorders such as upset stomachs, colic, and heartburn, as well as to induce a soothing sleep. Blessed with a strong, fragrant taste, dill seeds can be made into a tea.

SMOKED TROUT WITH DILL SAUCE

A light dinner for four—or a special appetizer for guests.

MAKES 4 SERVINGS

¼ cup spicy brown mustard
1 tablespoon honey
2 tablespoons fresh lemon juice
¼ cup capers
2 tablespoons fresh dill, chopped
¼ cup extra-virgin olive oil
  Freshly ground black pepper to taste
8 romaine lettuce leaves, washed and trimmed
1 pound smoked trout
  Lemon wedges and dill sprigs, for garnish

Step 1. Mix first five ingredients in a bowl. Slowly stir in oil.

Step 2. Season with crushed black pepper.

Step 3. Place lettuce in center of individual plates. Arrange equal amounts of fish on top of leaves.

Step 4. Pour sauce over fish and lettuce leaves, garnishing with lemon wedges and dill. Serve with Westphalian-style pumpernickel bread or crackers.

OTHER OPTIONS: Substitute other smoked fish for trout, such as salmon or even smoked oysters and sardines.

SNAPPER CRUNCH

We've added pumpkin seeds, which are loaded with vital omega-3 oil for an extra boost.

MAKES 4 SERVINGS

2 tablespoons anise seeds
¼ cup flax flour
1 teaspoon salt
1 cup shelled pepitas or pumpkin seeds, toasted
½ cup soy flour
2 large eggs

4 **red snapper fillets, 6 ounces each**
1 **tablespoon extra-virgin olive oil**
   Lemon wedges, for garnish

Step 1. Heat a small skillet over medium heat and add anise seeds. Toast for 2 minutes. Transfer seeds to a blender and blend at high speed.

Step 2. Add flax flour, salt, and pepitas to blender and pulse until coarsely chopped. Transfer mixture to baking sheet.

Step 3. Place soy flour on a separate plate.

Step 4. Beat eggs in a medium bowl. Dust both sides of each fillet with soy flour, then dip into egg.

Step 5. Coat both sides of snapper with pumpkin seed mixture.

Step 6. Heat 1 tablespoon of olive oil in a large skillet and sauté fillets. Turn and cook until golden, at least 3 minutes.

Step 7. Serve with lemon wedge garnish.

OTHER OPTIONS: Try substituting your favorite fish for the snapper.

SIMPLY SMASHING SNAPPER

A sizzling delight.

MAKES 2 SERVINGS

2 **snapper fillets, 6 ounces each**
3 **tablespoons red wine**
1 **tablespoon extra-virgin olive oil**
4–5 **garlic cloves, pressed**
4–5 **shallots, chopped**
   Juice of ½ lemon
2 **generous teaspoons fresh oregano, chopped**
2 **teaspoons fresh basil, chopped**
1 **teaspoon fresh parsley, chopped**
1 **tablespoon mango or papaya juice**

Step 1. Put snapper in marinade dish and cover with 2 tablespoons wine. Marinate overnight or at least 30 minutes in the refrigerator.

Step 2. Heat oil in a skillet, then toss in garlic and shallots. Sauté until translucent.

Step 3. Add snapper. Pour lemon juice over each fillet, then sprinkle with half the herbs. Let cook for 3 to 4 minutes, then turn fillets and sprinkle with remaining herbs.

Step 4. Continue cooking. When nearly done, pour in the last tablespoon of wine and a light splash of mango or papaya juice.

COCONUT SALMON

East meets West. We've choreographed coconut with salmon for a memorable performance.

MAKES 4 SERVINGS

1	tablespoon high-oleic safflower oil
1	medium red onion, chopped
2	garlic cloves, pressed
1	14-ounce can unsweetened light coconut milk
1	cup Chicken Stock (page 77)
½–1	teaspoon red curry paste, depending on desired spiciness
4	salmon fillets, 5 ounces each
	Salt and pepper to taste
2	medium carrots, cut julienne
1	medium zucchini, cut julienne
1	medium summer squash, cut julienne
4	scallions, thinly sliced, for garnish

Step 1. Preheat broiler for fish. Warm oil in a medium saucepan over medium heat.

Step 2. Add onions and garlic, sautéing until onion is translucent.

Step 3. Mix in coconut milk and stock. Add curry paste, then bring to a boil.

Step 4. Reduce heat and cook until liquid becomes slightly creamy, about 20 minutes.

Step 5. Meanwhile, place salmon on baking sheet. Season to taste, then broil until it turns opaque, about 10 minutes.

Step 6. Add carrots, zucchini, and squash to creamy mixture and cook until tender-crisp, about 5 minutes.

Step 7. Place salmon on serving plates and spoon sauce over fish. Top with scallions.

SASSY SALMON BURGERS

Forget the drive-thru: Try these snappy burgers. Exceptionally good when topped with Tangy Tapenade (page 62) or Pico de Gallo (page 67).

MAKES 4 SERVINGS

1 12-ounce can salmon, well drained
½ cup scallions, chopped
½ cup flax flour
¼ cup yellow cornmeal
4 tablespoons Spectrum Naturals organic mayonnaise
1 large egg, beaten
1 tablespoon Dijon mustard
1 tablespoon celery, finely chopped
   Salt and pepper to taste
¼ cup sesame seeds
1 tablespoon coriander seeds
1 tablespoon extra-virgin olive oil

Step 1. Place salmon in a large bowl and separate with a fork.

Step 2. Mix in next seven ingredients. Season to taste.

Step 3. Shape mixture into four patties, ¾-inch thick.

Step 4. Mix sesame seeds with coriander seeds, then dip patties into seed mixture, coating both sides.

Step 5. Heat oil in a large skillet over medium heat. Add salmon patties and cook until firm, about 4 minutes per side.

Step 6. Place patties on serving plates and top with aioli or dip.

ROASTED SALMON

Sinfully delicious!

MAKES 4 SERVINGS

3 tablespoons extra-virgin olive oil
4 salmon fillets, 5 ounces each
  Salt and pepper to taste
2 tablespoons fresh dill, chopped
1 large red onion, thinly sliced
2 tablespoons currant or grape juice
2 tablespoons balsamic vinegar
2 tablespoons slivered almonds, toasted

Step 1. Preheat oven to 400°F. Oil a baking dish with 1 tablespoon olive oil.

Step 2. Arrange salmon in center of dish and season to taste; then sprinkle with 1 tablespoon chopped dill.

Step 3. Roast until salmon is opaque in the center, about 10 minutes.

Step 4. Place 2 tablespoons oil in a medium pan over medium heat, and sauté onions until translucent.

Step 5. Add currant or grape juice and vinegar. Stir until mixture caramelizes. Set aside.

Step 6. Transfer salmon to serving dishes, top with currant sauce, and garnish with slivered almonds and the remaining dill.

SIZZLING SALMON

A fragrant sensation from North Africa.

MAKES 4 SERVINGS

2 tablespoons fresh lime juice
  Pinch of saffron threads, steeped in warm water for at least 4 minutes
3 tablespoons fresh Italian parsley, chopped
3 tablespoons fresh cilantro, chopped
2 garlic cloves, minced

2 teaspoons ground cumin
1 teaspoon allspice
Salt and pepper to taste
6 tablespoons extra-virgin olive oil
4 salmon fillets, 5 ounces each
½ cup blanched almonds, finely chopped, for garnish

Step 1. Combine first nine ingredients in a bowl.

Step 2. Place salmon fillets in a glass baking dish and spoon half the marinade over them. Turn to coat fish on both sides.

Step 3. Refrigerate and marinate at least 1 hour.

Step 4. Heat broiler. Place fish under broiler and cook for 4 minutes. Turn and cook for another 4 minutes or until opaque in the center.

Step 5. Serve immediately with remaining marinade drizzled on top. Garnish with almonds.

GRILLED SALMON

A delicate touch of the Mediterranean.

MAKES 4 SERVINGS

¼ cup extra-virgin olive oil
1 tablespoon fresh rosemary, or 1 teaspoon dried rosemary leaves
4 black peppercorns, whole
1 bay leaf
5 garlic cloves, pressed
4 salmon fillets, 5 ounces each
2 tablespoons extra-virgin olive oil
1 tablespoon apple cider vinegar
1 garlic clove, pressed
10 black olives, pitted and chopped
1 large tomato, seeded and chopped
½ red onion, thinly sliced
2 tablespoons capers, drained
Salt and pepper to taste

Step 1. Whisk first five ingredients in a small bowl.

Step 2. Place fish in a single layer in a glass baking dish.

Step 3. Pour oil mixture over fish, and turn fish to coat. Cover and refrigerate at least 4 hours.

Step 4. Whisk 2 tablespoons oil, vinegar, and garlic in a large bowl. Add olives, tomato, red onion, and capers.

Step 5. Prepare grill or preheat broiler. Season fish to taste. Grill or broil until salmon is opaque in center, about 8 to 10 minutes.

Step 6. Transfer to serving plates and top with tomato mixture. Serve immediately.

BASIL

Originating in India, this tasty herb has been used for centuries for healing. As a tea, it has been hailed as a sedative. Its soothing effects are said to help alleviate headaches as well as bad breath. Basil also possesses compounds to help combat arthritis and emphysema, plus antiviral substances that effectively fight warts.

SALMON AND EGGPLANT TANGO*

A tempting dance of flavors that'll have you kicking up your heels.

MAKES 2 SERVINGS

2 tablespoons extra-virgin olive oil
1 large onion, chopped
1 large green bell pepper, finely chopped
2–3 celery stalks, finely chopped
1 eggplant, peeled and cut into small cubes
1 8-ounce salmon fillet, skinned and cut into small pieces
Juice of 1 lemon
2 teaspoons fresh oregano, chopped
4 large garlic cloves, pressed
1 teaspoon fresh basil, chopped
Salt and pepper to taste
½ cup walnuts, chopped

Step 1. Warm olive oil in skillet, then add onion, bell pepper, and celery, sautéing until onion is translucent.

Step 2. Add eggplant and cook until tender.

Step 3. Add salmon pieces, then pour lemon juice over mixture and stir.

Step 4. Add herbs, seasonings, and walnuts. Cook until salmon is done, stirring frequently. (Add a little water, if needed, during cooking.)

*CARB ALERT: One serving equals 17 carbohydrate grams.

SALMON KEBOBS*

A colorful skewer of fun—great on the barbecue.

MAKES 4 SERVINGS

1   16-ounce salmon fillet, cut into medium cubes
2   teaspoons fresh oregano, chopped
4   large garlic cloves, pressed
1   teaspoon fresh dill, chopped
    Salt and pepper to taste
    Juice of ½ lemon
4   metal or wooden skewers
8   medium-size mushrooms, cleaned
1   pineapple, peeled and cut into chunks, or 1 can pineapple in large chunks
1   small basket cherry tomatoes
1   Vidalia onion, cut into chunks
2   green bell peppers, seeded and cut into wide slices

Step 1. Prepare the grill.

Step 2. Toss salmon cubes with herbs, seasonings, and lemon juice.

Step 3. Skewer salmon and remaining ingredients in any order you like. For example: 1 mushroom, 2 salmon pieces, 1 chunk pineapple, 1 tomato, 1 chunk onion, 1 salmon piece, 2 pieces pepper, 1 chunk pineapple.

*CARB ALERT: One serving equals 14 carbohydrate grams.

SAUCY SCALLOPS

These are the best with Minty Mashed Cauliflower (page 117) on the side.

MAKES 4 SERVINGS

1½ pounds sea scallops, rinsed
Salt and pepper to taste
2 tablespoons sesame oil
6 large shallots, chopped
4 tablespoons fresh basil, chopped
4 cups baby spinach leaves
⅔ cup white wine
½ cup plain low-fat yogurt
4 tablespoons pine nuts, toasted

Step 1. Sprinkle scallops with salt and pepper.

Step 2. Heat 1 tablespoon oil in a medium skillet and sauté scallops until opaque (about 6 minutes).

Step 3. Add half of the shallots and basil. Increase heat and add half the spinach. Toss.

Step 4. Add remaining spinach and toss until wilted. Divide onto plates.

Step 5. Place the remaining tablespoon of oil into the pan, and add the remaining shallots and basil. Sauté.

Step 6. Add wine and yogurt, then boil until the sauce is thick. Season with salt and pepper.

Step 7. Return scallops to skillet and simmer for 1 minute. Arrange scallops with sauce on top of spinach on individual serving plates. Sprinkle each serving with 1 tablespoon toasted pine nuts.

SCALLOP RHAPSODY

A symphonic medley that gets a standing ovation every time.

MAKES 3 SERVINGS

1–2 tablespoons extra-virgin olive oil
1 pound sea scallops
Juice of ½ lemon
1½ teaspoons fresh oregano, chopped
3 large garlic cloves, pressed
1 teaspoon fresh parsley, chopped
1 teaspoon fresh basil, chopped
1 tablespoon mango juice
Lemon wedges, for garnish

Step 1. Pour oil into skillet and heat. Add scallops, turning lightly.

Step 2. Sprinkle with lemon juice and herbs. Let simmer for 1 to 2 minutes.

Step 3. Add mango juice and simmer for 2 to 3 minutes more. Serve with lemon-wedge garnish.

CRAB CAKE CASSEROLE*

Busy night? Try this easy dish. It's terrific with a side of tossed greens and a medley of your favorite veggies.

MAKES 4 SERVINGS

½ pound cooked crabmeat
2 celery stalks, finely chopped
1 red bell pepper, diced
⅓ cup black olives, minced
¼ cup fresh cilantro, finely chopped
1 medium onion, minced
2 large garlic cloves, pressed
1 teaspoon fresh basil, chopped
1 teaspoon fresh oregano, chopped
Salt and pepper to taste
Dash of cayenne pepper
1 egg

1 cup bread crumbs
1 cup plain low-fat yogurt
Juice of ½ lemon
1 tablespoon extra-virgin olive oil

Step 1. Preheat oven to 400°F. Mix crab, celery, pepper, olives, cilantro, onion, and seasonings in a bowl.

Step 2. Whisk egg in a separate bowl and blend with bread crumbs, yogurt, and lemon juice.

Step 3. Gradually stir egg mixture into crab mixture.

Step 4. Place in a lightly oiled casserole dish. Bake for 15 to 20 minutes at 400°F.

*CARB ALERT: One serving equals 18 carbohydrate grams.

VINO SHRIMP SAUTÉ

Simple, yet delectable.

MAKES 3 TO 4 SERVINGS

1–2 tablespoons extra-virgin olive oil
4–5 garlic cloves, pressed
1 pound shrimp
1 teaspoon fresh basil, chopped
2 teaspoons fresh oregano, chopped
1 teaspoon fresh parsley, chopped
Salt and pepper to taste
Dash of cayenne pepper
2 tablespoons red or white wine
Lemon wedges, for garnish

Step 1. Warm oil in a skillet; then sauté garlic.

Step 2. Toss in shrimp. Stir.

Step 3. Add herbs and seasonings and simmer for 1 minute or so.

Step 4. Just before shrimp turns opaque, pour in 2 tablespoons wine and simmer 2 minutes longer. Serve with lemon-wedge garnish.

COCO-NUTTY SHRIMP

This crunchy treat will remind you of Aruba, Bonaire, and Curaçao.

MAKES 4 SERVINGS

1	cup fresh cilantro, chopped
½	cup unsweetened light coconut milk
4	garlic cloves, pressed
2	tablespoons fresh lime juice
2	teaspoons fish sauce (nam pla)
1½	pounds large shrimp, peeled and deveined
⅓	cup crunchy peanut butter
¼	cup Chicken Stock (page 77)
2	tablespoons unsweetened light coconut milk
4	garlic cloves, pressed
2	teaspoons fresh lime juice
1	tablespoon fresh ginger, minced
1	teaspoon soy sauce
1	teaspoon fish sauce (nam pla)
½	teaspoon red curry paste
4	metal skewers

Step 1. Prepare shrimp marinade by blending cilantro, coconut milk, garlic, lime juice, ginger, and fish sauce (available at health food stores) in a food processor.

Step 2. Place shrimp in a large glass baking dish and add marinade. Cover and refrigerate for at least 2 hours.

Step 3. About 30 minutes before you're ready to cook the shrimp, make the peanut sauce: Purée next nine ingredients in food processor until smooth. Set aside.

Step 4. Preheat broiler. Thread shrimp onto skewers and broil until cooked through, about 2 minutes per side.

Step 5. Serve shrimp skewers with peanut sauce.

GRILLED TUNA STEAKS

A taste of Italy, with an omega twist.

MAKES 4 SERVINGS

Omega Star Pesto (pages 63 to 64)
4 tuna steaks, 5 ounces each
Salt and pepper to taste

Step 1. Heat grill or broiler. If pesto isn't already prepared, make the mixture now.

Step 2. Season tuna to taste, then grill until the middle is opaque.

Step 3. Transfer fish to plates and top with pesto.

TUNA AND SALSA SUPREME

Want a break from the ho-hum? This dish has a bold attitude that'll turn heads.

MAKES 4 SERVINGS

½ cup fresh parsley, chopped
¼ cup extra-virgin olive oil
2 tablespoons scallions, chopped
2 tablespoons fresh lime juice
2 garlic cloves, pressed
1 teaspoon fresh sage, chopped
1 teaspoon fresh savory, chopped
1 teaspoon fresh basil, chopped
Salt and pepper to taste
4 tuna steaks, 5 ounces each
1 tablespoon extra-virgin olive oil
Dill sprigs, for garnish
Lemon slices, for garnish

Step 1. Heat oven to 350°F.

Step 2. For Salsa Verde: Mix the first nine ingredients in a medium bowl. Set aside.

Step 3. Pat tuna steaks with paper towels. Season to taste.

Step 4. Oil a large baking sheet. Place steaks on the sheet, then top with Salsa Verde and bake until tuna is opaque in the center, about 10 to 12 minutes.

Step 5. Garnish plates with dill sprigs and lemon slices. Serve immediately.

OUTRAGEOUS TUNA BURGERS*

Tired of hamburgers? Try this tempting alternative.

MAKES 4 SERVINGS

1   12-ounce can solid white tuna packed in water, well drained
½   cup scallions, chopped
½   cup flax flour
¼   cup yellow cornmeal
4   tablespoons Spectrum Naturals organic mayonnaise
1   large egg, beaten
1   tablespoon horseradish
1   tablespoon celery, finely chopped
    Salt and pepper to taste
1   tablespoon extra-virgin olive oil
4   leaves romaine lettuce
4   slices tomato

Step 1. Place tuna in a large bowl and separate with fork.

Step 2. Mix in scallions, flaxseed flour, cornmeal, mayonnaise, egg, horseradish, celery, and seasonings.

Step 3. Shape mixture into four generous silver-dollar-sized patties.

Step 4. Heat oil in a large skillet over medium heat. Add tuna patties and cook until firm, about 4 minutes per side.

Step 5. Place patties on serving plates and top with lettuce and tomato.

*CARB ALERT: One serving equals 10 carbohydrate grams.

Meats and Poultry

It's what they've all been waiting for—the star of the show, the entrée. You want it to be filling, appetizing, and nutritionally sound. And with all of these dishes, that's exactly what you'll get. They sound good, taste even better, and are all quite simple to make. So even a novice cook can pull off a showcase meal.

What's more, they provide you and your family with protein power. And having protein power means your energy levels stay high longer, your blood sugar levels stay in balance, your immune system is strengthened, and the healing process is bolstered. Most important, your body's fat-burning capabilities are stimulated. We've given you our version of numerous fav orites from the home front and across the globe: Stuffed Peppers, Southwest Salisbury Steaks, Cashew Chicken, Cuban-Style Turkey Breast, and Three-Step Veal Cutlets, to name just a few.

With so many choices, what are you in the mood for tonight?

Beef

No need to banish red meat from your diet. Just be sure to buy lean cuts that are certified as being fed natural grains, without antibiotics or growth stimulants. Then get ready to enjoy these tantalizing meals.

STUFFED PEPPERS

Just like Grandma used to make.

MAKES 4 TO 6 SERVINGS

2 pounds lean ground chuck
1 potato, grated
   Salt and pepper to taste
4–5 green bell peppers, cut in half with seeds scooped out
1 26-ounce jar Classico Roasted Garlic Sauce
1 8-ounce can mushrooms with liquid
1–2 garlic cloves, minced

Step 1. Combine hamburger, grated potato, and seasonings.

Step 2. Put a scoop into each pepper and place peppers right side up in a 2-quart Pyrex baking dish.

Step 3. Blend sauce, mushrooms, and garlic together, then pour mixture over peppers.

Step 4. Bake covered at 350°F for 1¼ hours.

ASIAN STIR-FRY

A Far East wonder, rich in health-boosting—and waist-slimming—fats.
Try substituting fish, poultry, or even tofu for the beef.

MAKES 4 SERVINGS

    1 tablespoon low-sodium tamari
    1 tablespoon fresh ginger, grated
    1 teaspoon sesame oil
    1 tablespoon unsweetened peanut butter
 1¼ pounds petit sirloin steaks, well trimmed and cut into strips
    1 pound string beans, trimmed
    2 teaspoons high-oleic safflower oil
  ⅓ cup fresh orange juice
    1 teaspoon apple cider vinegar
    1 teaspoon agar-agar or arrowroot
    1 teaspoon fresh orange zest
    1 garlic clove, pressed
  ¼ cup almonds, chopped and roasted, for garnish

Step 1. Mix first four ingredients in a glass baking dish. Add meat and let marinate for at least 1 hour.

Step 2. Meanwhile, cook beans in a large pot of boiling water for 3 to 5 minutes. Drain.

Step 3. Heat a large skillet and add 1 teaspoon oil. Toss in beef and sauté until medium done.

Step 4. Transfer beef to a plate and wipe the skillet clean.

Step 5. Whisk juice, vinegar, agar-agar, orange zest, and garlic in a small bowl.

Step 6. Heat 1 teaspoon oil in the same skillet over medium heat. Add string beans and sauté briefly.

Step 7. Add meat and orange juice mixture, letting sauce come to a boil as you stir to coat the meat. Garnish with almonds.

FLAVORFUL FLANK STEAK

All spiced up and only one place to go—your broiler! The oregano, coriander,
and garlic are all potent immunity boosters.

MAKES 4 SERVINGS

1   tablespoon ground cumin
½   tablespoon chili powder
1   teaspoon dried oregano
½   teaspoon ground coriander
½   teaspoon ground black pepper
2   large garlic cloves, pressed
1   tablespoon extra-virgin olive oil
1¼   pounds flank steak
    Salt and pepper to taste
4   lemon wedges, for garnish
4   tablespoons peanuts, chopped, for garnish
2   tablespoons fresh cilantro, chopped, for garnish

Step 1. Blend first seven ingredients in a small bowl to form a paste.

Step 2. Rub mixture over steak, then transfer to a baking dish and refrigerate for about 2 hours.

Step 3. Heat broiler (or prepare outdoor grill). Season steak with salt and pepper.

Step 4. Cook until desired doneness (5 minutes per side for medium).

Step 5. Place on cutting board and cut against the grain into ½-inch strips.

Step 6. Transfer to serving plate and garnish with lemon, chopped peanuts, and cilantro.

SOUTHWEST SALISBURY STEAKS

A zesty version of the all-time favorite.

MAKES 4 SERVINGS

1¼ pounds ground sirloin
¼ cup fresh cilantro, chopped
¼ cup mild green chilis, chopped
2 tablespoons scallions, finely chopped
3 tablespoons low-sodium salsa
1 teaspoon chili powder
1 teaspoon ground cumin
¼ cup flax flour
  Salt and pepper to taste
1 California avocado, peeled and quartered

Step 1. Prepare grill or broiler.

Step 2. Place all ingredients except avocado in a large bowl and blend by hand. Shape into ¾-inch oval patties.

Step 3. Grill for 7 minutes per side.

Step 4. Transfer to plates and serve with avocado.

COMPANY MEATLOAF

Who says classics can't be improved?

MAKES 4 SERVINGS

2 teaspoons extra-virgin olive oil
1¼ pounds lean ground sirloin
1 cup scallions, thinly cut
½ cup low-sodium salsa
1 egg
¼ cup flax flour
1 tablespoon chili powder
  Salt and pepper to taste
3 tablespoons salsa, for topping

Step 1. Preheat oven to 350°F. Oil an 8-inch baking dish with extra-virgin olive oil.

Step 2. Combine beef, scallions, ½ cup salsa, egg, flour, chili powder, salt, and pepper in a bowl.

Step 3. Blend well and shape into a loaf. Set into baking dish.

Step 4. Spread the remaining 3 tablespoons salsa over loaf and bake uncovered for about 20 minutes.

Step 5. Let cool and cut loaf into four slices. Serve immediately.

MAMA'S MEATLOAF

Real comfort food straight from Mama Edith's Kitchen.

MAKES 5 TO 6 SERVINGS

1 tablespoon extra-virgin olive oil

2 pounds ground chuck (or 1 pound lean chuck plus 1 pound veal)

1 cup seasoned bread crumbs

¾ cup onions, chopped

2 tablespoons horseradish

2 teaspoons salt (optional)

¼ teaspoon pepper

1 teaspoon dry mustard

½ cup ketchup

2 eggs, slightly beaten

Step 1. Preheat oven to 350°F. Oil an 8 × 4 × 2-inch Pyrex loaf pan with extra-virgin olive oil.

Step 2. Combine rest of ingredients, blending by hand.

Step 3. Shape and set in loaf dish. Bake for 1¼ hours.

SHEPHERD'S PIE*

*This delicious dish brings back some wonderful family memories. Yes, it contains
potatoes . . . but it's so good, it's worth adjusting your daily carbohydrate intake.
Try a nice green salad as an accompaniment.*

MAKES 6 TO 8 SERVINGS

8 potatoes (whipped with Chicken Stock, if desired)
2 tablespoons high-oleic safflower oil
2 medium carrots, diced
2 medium celery stalks, diced
1 large onion, diced
1 medium green bell pepper, cored and peeled
2 garlic cloves, pressed
1½ pounds lean ground beef
1 teaspoon dried thyme leaves
1 teaspoon dried oregano
½ teaspoon dried basil leaves
½ teaspoon black pepper
1 8-ounce can tomato sauce
2 tablespoons ketchup
1 tablespoon Worcestershire sauce
Salt to taste
¼ cup fresh parsley, chopped

Step 1. Cook potatoes, mash, then set aside.

Step 2. In a 12-inch skillet, heat oil and add carrots, celery, onion, green
pepper, and garlic. Cook about 3 minutes, stirring until veggies
are tender-crisp.

Step 3. Add ground beef, herbs, and seasonings. Cook for 5 minutes.

Step 4. Add tomato sauce, ketchup, and Worcestershire sauce, salt, and
parsley, bringing to a boil and stirring constantly.

Step 5. Reduce heat and let simmer for about 5 minutes until flavors
blend.

Step 6. Remove from pan and place in a 3-quart Pyrex dish.

Step 7. Spoon mashed potatoes on top of meat and bake for 1½ hours
at 350°F.

*CARB ALERT: One serving equals 21 to 24 carbohydrate grams.

Chicken

Rekindle your family's love for chicken with these inventive recipes. Be sure to choose natural, free-range chicken, raised without antibiotics or growth stimulants.

ROSEMARY

Brimming with antioxidants, this member of the mint family has long been associated with memory improvement. It's also known for preventing heart disease and cataracts as well as aiding arthritis, body aches, and even healthy hair. The herb's oil is often used to treat depression since it contains a compound that stimulates the central nervous system.

LEMON-WALNUT CHICKEN

A tangy favorite at any dinner table.

MAKES 4 SERVINGS

¾ cup white wine
   Juice of 2 large lemons, plus zest
4 garlic cloves, pressed
1 large Vidalia onion, chopped
1 tablespoon fresh rosemary, chopped
1 tablespoon fresh oregano, chopped
1 tablespoon fresh basil, chopped
   Salt and pepper to taste
4 boneless chicken breast halves
2 tablespoons extra-virgin olive oil
½ cup Chicken Stock (page 77) blended with 2 teaspoons agar-agar or arrowroot
   Paprika, for garnish
¼ cup crushed walnuts, for garnish

Step 1. Whisk wine and lemon juice together. Stir in lemon zest, garlic, onions, herbs, and seasonings.

Step 2. Place chicken in a glass container. Marinate in wine mixture, refrigerating for no more than 2 hours.

Step 3. Remove chicken from marinade and pat dry. Save marinade.

Step 4. In a skillet, heat olive oil and sauté chicken on both sides until done. Remove chicken; set aside in a warm place.

Step 5. Pour marinade into skillet. Over high heat, simmer until liquid reduces to half. Then add Chicken Stock–agar-agar mixture to create a slightly thicker sauce.

Step 6. Pour mixture over each chicken breast. Sprinkle with paprika and crushed walnuts.

CHICKEN FAJITAS*

We've dressed up this quick and tasty dish with a velvety avocado salsa.

MAKES 4 SERVINGS

1 large tomato, seeded and chopped
1 California avocado, diced
½ cup tomatillos, husked, seeded, and chopped
½ red onion, chopped
½ cup fresh cilantro, chopped
½ small jalapeño pepper, seeded and chopped
2 tablespoons extra-virgin olive oil
2 tablespoons fresh lime juice
Salt and pepper to taste
1 tablespoon ground cumin
2 teaspoons chili powder
4 chicken breasts, 5 ounces each, skin removed, cut into ½-inch strips
1 tablespoon extra-virgin olive oil
1 red bell pepper, cut julienne
1 green bell pepper, cut julienne
1 tablespoon fresh lime juice
4 corn tortillas

Step 1. Mix first eight ingredients in a bowl for salsa. Season to taste. Refrigerate until ready to use.

Step 2. In a separate bowl, blend cumin, chili powder, salt, and pepper.

Step 3. Dip chicken strips into cumin mixture until coated.

Step 4. Heat oil in a skillet and sauté chicken. Add bell peppers and stir.

Step 5. Pour in lime juice and cook chicken until done, about 7 to 10 minutes.

Step 6. Serve chicken topped with avocado salsa. Accompany each serving with a tortilla.

*CARB ALERT: One serving equals 22 carbohydrate grams.

GREEK CHICKEN

This delicious recipe comes from the Greek isles, where the inhabitants are trim and healthy.

MAKES 2 SERVINGS

1 **large lemon**
3 **tablespoons fresh parsley, chopped**
1 **teaspoon dried oregano**
Salt and pepper to taste
2 **garlic cloves, pressed**
2 **tablespoons extra-virgin olive oil**
2 **5-ounce chicken breasts with skin and bones**
1 **tablespoon Kalamata olives, chopped**
½ **cup plain nonfat yogurt**

Step 1. Grate lemon over a large bowl. Then cut in half and squeeze the juice from one half. Save the other half.

Step 2. Add parsley, oregano, salt, pepper, garlic, and oil.

Step 3. Place chicken in a bowl and rub with citrus-herb mixture. Let marinate for at least 1 hour in the refrigerator.

Step 4. Preheat broiler.

Step 5. Place chicken under broiler and cook for approximately 15 minutes per side until chicken is thoroughly cooked.

Step 6. Meanwhile, create topping by blending the juice of the remaining lemon half with the chopped olives and yogurt. When chicken is done, serve with a dollop of yogurt sauce.

CRUNCHY CHICKEN

Hankering for something crispy? Here's a good choice, inspired by Southwest ingredients. Jicama Slaw, featured on page 107, makes a tasty companion and adds more omega oils to the meal.

MAKES 4 SERVINGS

¼ cup yellow cornmeal
2 teaspoons ground cumin
4 5-ounce skinless, boneless chicken breasts
   Salt and pepper to taste
1 tablespoon extra-virgin olive oil

Step 1. Preheat oven to 250°F. Mix cornmeal and cumin in a shallow bowl.

Step 2. Sprinkle chicken with salt and pepper, then coat with cornmeal mixture.

Step 3. Put oil in a pan and warm over medium-low heat. Sauté chicken breasts until golden brown. Turn chicken over and cook until thoroughly done.

Step 4. Transfer chicken pieces to a baking sheet and place in a warm oven until ready to serve.

CASHEW CHICKEN

This colorful dish is a breeze to fix and ever so satisfying.

MAKES 4 SERVINGS

¼ cup Chicken Stock (page 77)
1 tablespoon low-sodium soy sauce
3 tablespoons dry sherry
1 tablespoon agar-agar or arrowroot
2 tablespoons walnut oil
2 garlic cloves, pressed
1 tablespoon fresh ginger, grated
4 5-ounce chicken breasts, cut into ½-inch strips
2 cups broccoli florets
1 cup scallions, chopped
4 tablespoons cashews, chopped, for garnish

Step 1. For sauce, whisk first four ingredients in a small bowl until agar-agar dissolves. Set aside.

Step 2. Heat oil in a large skillet or wok. Sauté garlic and ginger, then add chicken and brown about 5 to 7 minutes.

Step 3. Add broccoli and scallions, sautéing for another 3 to 5 minutes.

Step 4. Pour sauce into mixture and bring to a boil, stirring until sauce thickens and gently coats ingredients, about 1 minute.

Step 5. Place chicken on serving plates. Top each serving with 1 tablespoon cashews.

MONDAY-NIGHT CHICKEN STIR-FRY

A savory, slimming dish . . . the key is in the marinade.

MAKES 4 SERVINGS

1 **pound chicken breast, cut in ½-inch strips**
2 **tablespoons jerk seasoning**
1 **tablespoon fresh lime juice**
2 **teaspoons sesame seed oil**
1 **garlic clove, pressed**
1 **teaspoon fresh ginger, grated**
3 **scallions, chopped**
1 **celery stalk, chopped**
1 **zucchini, cut julienne**
1 **red bell pepper, cut julienne**
1 **green bell pepper, cut julienne**
1 **yellow bell pepper, cut julienne**
½ **pound mushrooms, sliced**
½ **teaspoon hot sauce**
4 **tablespoons peanuts**

Step 1. Place chicken in a bowl. Add jerk seasoning and lime juice. Let marinate for at least 4 hours.

Step 2. Place oil in a large skillet over medium heat. Add chicken strips and marinade.

Step 3. Brown chicken on both sides, then add garlic, ginger, and scallions. Stir.

Step 4. Add vegetables and hot sauce, and stir. Let cook for another 8 to 10 minutes.

Step 5. Place on serving plates. Top each serving with 1 tablespoon peanuts.

BBQ CHICKEN

Finger-licking good. The high-omega almond flour replaces the usual high-carb flour thickener.

MAKES 4 SERVINGS

2 teaspoons extra-virgin olive oil
¼ cup almonds, blanched
4 skinless chicken breasts with bones
1 8-ounce can tomatoes, crushed
3 tablespoons tomato paste
½ cup fresh orange juice
2 tablespoons apple cider vinegar
½ teaspoon Worcestershire sauce
2 tablespoons honey mustard
Salt and pepper to taste

Step 1. Preheat oven to 350°F. Coat a Pyrex pan with oil.

Step 2. Process almonds in a food processor until consistency of flour.

Step 3. Dip chicken breasts into nut flour and coat.

Step 4. Place chicken in a Pyrex pan.

Step 5. In a medium saucepan, heat tomatoes, tomato paste, orange juice, apple cider vinegar, Worcestershire sauce, honey mustard, salt, and pepper. Boil for 1 minute, then lower heat and simmer sauce until it thickens, about 5 minutes.

Step 6. Pour sauce over chicken breasts. Cover and bake for 20 minutes. Remove cover and let chicken brown for another 15 to 20 minutes. Serve immediately.

Turkey

Don't wait until Thanksgiving to enjoy this delicious bird. These recipes take turkey to a whole new level.

WALNUT TURKEY BREAST

*Company for dinner? Wow your friends with this
surprisingly different, flaxy dish.*

MAKES 4 SERVINGS

¾ cup walnuts, chopped
½ cup flax flour
1 egg, beaten
1 tablespoon extra-virgin olive oil
4 turkey breast cutlets, 5 ounces each
¼ cup Marsala wine
2 tablespoons shallots, chopped
½ cup Chicken Stock (page 77)
¼ cup unsweetened cranberry juice
1½ teaspoons red currant or raspberry jam
    Salt and pepper to taste
2 tablespoons chives, chopped, for garnish
4 walnut halves, for garnish

Step 1. Chop walnuts in a food processor, then place in a bowl and mix with flax flour. Set aside.

Step 2. In a separate bowl, beat egg. Dip each cutlet into beaten egg, then into flax flour–walnut mix. Be sure to coat both sides.

Step 3. Heat oil in a large skillet. Add turkey and cook until golden, about 3 minutes per side. Transfer to a serving plate and keep warm.

Step 4. Simmer Marsala wine and shallots in a medium saucepan until wine evaporates, about 2 minutes.

Step 5. Add stock, cranberry juice, and jam. Stir, then boil for 1 minute. Lower heat and reduce sauce. Season to taste.

Step 6. Spoon sauce over turkey and sprinkle with chives. Garnish each cutlet with a walnut half.

CUBAN-STYLE TURKEY BREAST

Caribbean spices with a turkey twist. Top off each serving with some Black Bean and Peanut Salsa (featured on page 68).

MAKES 6 SERVINGS

½ cup fresh orange juice
¼ cup fresh lime juice
1 medium red onion, thinly sliced
2 teaspoons fresh oregano, chopped
2 teaspoons ground cumin
2 teaspoons salt
1 bay leaf, crumbled
½ teaspoon freshly ground black pepper
1 4- to 5-pound turkey breast with bone and skin
6 orange slices
6 lime slices
6 sprigs cilantro

Step 1. Mix first eight ingredients in a large resealable plastic bag.

Step 2. Add turkey breast to bag. Close bag and coat turkey breast with marinade. Refrigerate for at least 4 hours or overnight.

Step 3. Preheat oven to 325°F. Transfer turkey to a roasting pan, discarding marinade.

Step 4. Cover pan and bake until done, about 45 minutes. Uncover and increase temperature to 400°F. Let turkey brown for about 5 minutes. Remove from oven.

Step 5. Let stand for approximately 5 minutes before cutting.

Step 6. Arrange a 4-ounce piece of turkey on each dinner plate and garnish with slices of orange and lime and a cilantro sprig. If serving Black Bean and Peanut Salsa, spoon ¼ cup on top of the turkey breast before serving.

GARLIC

Back in the days of the Pharaohs, garlic was used to help heal infections and wounds. Since then, garlic has been touted for its power to reduce blood pressure, cholesterol, and mucus in the lungs as well as to fight viral infections. This megastar herb is also applauded for boosting the immune system and stimulating enzymatic activity in the liver to neutralize toxins.

APRICOT TURKEY BREAST*

Savory, yet simple to make—perfect for festive occasions.

MAKES 6 SERVINGS

1	3-pound turkey breast
6	garlic cloves
1	tablespoon extra-virgin olive oil
	Salt and pepper to taste
1	teaspoon fresh rosemary, chopped
1	teaspoon fresh basil, chopped
24	dried apricot halves
¾	cup dried cranberries
3	large carrots, cut into ½-inch slices
1	cup broccoli florets
1½	cups turkey broth
2	tablespoons white wine

Step 1. Preheat oven to 375°F. Make slits in turkey breast with a knife and insert a garlic clove in each one.

Step 2. Rub turkey breast with olive oil, then sprinkle with salt and pepper. Place turkey breast in a shallow roasting pan and season with rosemary and basil.

Step 3. Create a colorful nest around the turkey with apricots, cranberries, carrots, and broccoli.

Step 4. Lightly mix broth with wine and pour over fruit-veggie nest.

Step 5. Cover and bake for 45 minutes, or until meat is done, basting often.

*CARB ALERT: One serving equals 18 carbohydrate grams.

Lamb and Veal

Lamb and veal are tempting alternatives to poultry and beef. Moreover, lamb is the highest source of the amino acid L-carnitine, which helps to burn stored body fat for energy. We've combined just the right herbs to take out that "gamey" taste sometimes associated with these meats.

JUICY LEG OF LAMB

*An herbal delight—an easy meal anytime you want
something special with no fuss.*

MAKES 6 SERVINGS

1   boneless leg of lamb (approximately 3½ pounds)
5–6   garlic cloves, slivered
1–2   tablespoons extra-virgin olive oil
1   tablespoon fresh rosemary, chopped
1   tablespoon fresh basil, chopped
    Salt and pepper to taste
⅓   cup red wine

Step 1. Preheat oven to 375°F. Make slits in lamb with a knife and insert a garlic sliver in each one.

Step 2. Coat lamb with olive oil, then sprinkle with herbs and seasonings.

Step 3. Place lamb in a roasting pan and bake until done, approximately 20 minutes per pound. Baste often with pan drippings, pouring wine over lamb during last 30 minutes of cooking.

LAMB OR VEAL KEBOBS

All the exotic charm and flax-filled flavor of the Middle East are here. Add a salad and some Middle Eastern Hummus (featured on page 60) to enhance the mood.

MAKES 4 SERVINGS

1 **pound ground lamb or ground veal**
1 **medium onion, finely chopped**
¼ **cup flax flour**
¼ **teaspoon cayenne pepper**
½ **teaspoon ground cumin**
½ **teaspoon allspice**
2 **tablespoons fresh cilantro, finely chopped**
2 **tablespoons fresh lemon juice**
Salt and pepper to taste
4 **metal or wooden skewers**
4 **tablespoons sesame seeds**
1 **lemon, quartered, for garnish**

Step 1. Prepare barbecue or broiler.

Step 2. Place first nine ingredients in a large bowl. Mix well.

Step 3. Divide mixture into four equal parts. Take a skewer in one hand and a quarter of the meat mixture in the other. Firmly press the meat around the skewer like a small hot dog.

Step 4. Coat each one with sesame seeds.

Step 5. Cook for about 15 to 20 minutes, turning at least once. Garnish with lemon and serve.

THREE-STEP VEAL CUTLETS

Elegance was never so easy, or so appetizing.

MAKES 4 SERVINGS

1 tablespoon extra-virgin olive oil
4–5 garlic cloves, pressed
4–5 scallions, finely chopped
1 green bell pepper, cut julienne
1 pound veal cutlets, thinly sliced
2–3 tablespoons red wine
1 tablespoon fresh basil, chopped
1 tablespoon fresh oregano, chopped
Salt and pepper to taste
1 lemon, cut into 4 wedges, for garnish
Parsley sprigs, for garnish

Step 1. Heat oil in a skillet and sauté garlic, scallions, and green pepper.

Step 2. Add veal, wine, herbs, and seasonings. Brown on both sides, then simmer until done.

Step 3. Garnish with lemon and parsley.

Tasty Treats

The grand finale—to help finish special meals with flair. Let's face it. Kids—and most adults—can't live without sweets. Understandably, you've probably tried to keep sweet-snacking to a minimum since most dessert recipes are loaded with unhealthy fats and refined flour and sugar. But what if you could offer your family delectable omega-rich treats now and then? Everyone would be happy, right? Well, here they are: our healthy alternatives for the kid in all of us.

These healthy confections are fun to eat, too. Just munch one of our Peanut Butter Balls, made with coconut and carob, or our delectable Bran Fruit Bars, loaded with prunes, dates, figs, and raisins. And get out the spoons because our Yummy-in-Your-Tummy Pudding and Vanilla Tapioca are habit-forming!

Now you and your kids can have your sweets . . . and omegas, too.

Bars and Other Fun Snacks

Each one of these tantalizing morsels comforts that sweet tooth and helps keep your omega quotient high. What a lovely reward after a special meal, or just anytime.

BRAN FRUIT BARS*

Great for your kid's lunch box or midafternoon snack. Jade Beutler came up with this tasty treat, which appears in the Flax for Life *cookbook.*

MAKES 12 BARS

¼ pound pitted prunes
¼ pound dates
¼ pound figs
¼ pound raisins
¼ cup raw honey
3 tablespoons fresh lemon juice
3 tablespoons flax oil
1 cup bran
½ cup wheat germ
1 tablespoon fresh orange zest

Step 1. Process dried fruits in a food processor.

Step 2. In a separate bowl, mix honey, lemon juice, flax oil, bran, wheat germ, and orange zest.

Step 3. Blend the processed fruit with the honey mixture, mixing well.

Step 4. Press the mixture into a pan and refrigerate for up to 1 hour.

Step 5. Cut into bars and serve.

*CARB ALERT: One serving equals 26 carbohydrate grams.

NUTS GALORE

Almonds, walnuts, hazelnuts, and pistachios find their way into tempting sauces that enhance a multitude of Arabic meat dishes. Both the Arabs and the Turks feast on delicate nut-filled pastries coated in honey. And Eastern Europeans also make delicious baked goods with these nuts.

PEANUT BUTTER BALLS

Your family will love this yummy treat, another one of Jade Beutler's delicious ideas adapted from the Flax for Life *cookbook.*

MAKES 6 SERVINGS

½   cup natural crunchy peanut butter
½   cup flax oil
½   cup shredded coconut
½   cup carob powder

Step 1. Thoroughly mix peanut butter and flax oil in a bowl.

Step 2. Stir in coconut and carob powder. (If mixture isn't thick, add more coconut.)

Step 3. Form into balls.

Step 4. Serve immediately or cover and chill for later use.

FLAX SNAX BALLS

Looking for some munchies? Here's a fiber-rich treat with the lovable taste of cinnamon. It's adapted from Jade Beutler's recipe in the Flax for Life *cookbook.*

MAKES 24 1-INCH BALLS

¾   cup flax flour
3   tablespoons oat flour
1½ teaspoons cinnamon
1   teaspoon ground cardamom
2   tablespoons unsweetened crunchy peanut butter
½   cup brown rice syrup
    Coconut flakes, as needed
6   tablespoons almonds, ground

Step 1. Mix flax flour, oat flour, cinnamon, and cardamom in a bowl.

Step 2. Blend in peanut butter and rice syrup, then knead by hand.

Step 3. Tear off pieces and roll into 1-inch balls. (Or roll dough into a log and slice.)

Step 4. Sprinkle coconut flakes and ground almonds on waxed paper, then roll balls (or slices) in the mixture.

Step 5. Serve immediately or chill for later use.

TOFRUITY YOGURT*

*Want a switch from yogurt? Here it is, and it's enriched with flax oil to boot—
another sweet delight from Jade Beutler's* Flax for Life *cookbook.*

MAKES 3 SERVINGS

1   12-ounce block silken tofu
1½ cups chopped frozen strawberries, blueberries, or raspberries
2   tablespoons flax oil
2   teaspoons nonalcohol vanilla extract
2   teaspoons raw honey

Combine ingredients (in order listed above) in food processor or blender,
and process to an even consistency.

*CARB ALERT: One serving equals 18 carbohydrate grams.

Puddings

Remember those sweet memories of spooning up Grandma's creamy home-
made pudding? You felt loved with every bite. With these inviting recipes,
you can re-create those feelings for your own family and friends.

YUMMY-IN-YOUR-TUMMY PUDDING*

*Sweet, smooth, and luscious . . . my six-year-old nephew Isaac loved
this creamy pudding so much, he named it!*

MAKES 4 SERVINGS

2   cups almond milk
3   tablespoons agar-agar or arrowroot
3   tablespoons honey
1   egg
¼   teaspoon almond extract
½   teaspoon cinnamon
    Toasted flaxseeds

Step 1. Heat 1½ cups almond milk on low.

Step 2. Meanwhile, dissolve agar-agar in remaining ½ cup almond milk, then add to saucepan and bring to a gentle boil, stirring constantly.

Step 3. Reduce heat and add honey, mixing thoroughly.

Step 4. Whisk egg in a separate bowl, then add 1 cup of cooled pudding mixture and stir.

Step 5. Pour egg mixture into the saucepan and stir constantly, thoroughly mixing all ingredients.

Step 6. Let boil, stirring constantly. Remove from heat and mix in almond extract and cinnamon.

Step 7. Let cool for 20 minutes. Refrigerate and serve chilled with toasted flaxseeds sprinkled on top.

*CARB ALERT: One serving equals 23 carbohydrate grams.

VANILLA TAPIOCA*

Is there anything more satisfying than the taste of vanilla blended into the rich texture of tapioca? Here's a spin-off from a popular tapioca pudding that appeared in my first book, Beyond Pritikin.

MAKES 4 SERVINGS

3 tablespoons granulated tapioca
1½ cups almond milk
½ teaspoon salt (optional)
3 tablespoons honey
1 egg
1 teaspoon nonalcohol vanilla extract
Toasted flaxseeds

Step 1. Heat tapioca, almond milk, and salt (if desired) on low.

Step 2. Bring to a slow boil, cooking uncovered for 5 minutes and stirring frequently.

Step 3. Reduce heat and add honey, blending thoroughly.

Step 4. Whisk egg in a separate bowl, then add 1 cup of partially cooled pudding mixture.

Step 5. Pour egg mixture into the saucepan and stir constantly, bringing to a boil.

Step 6. Simmer for 3 minutes over low heat. Remove from stove and add vanilla extract.

Step 7. Let cool for 20 minutes. Refrigerate and serve chilled with toasted flaxseeds sprinkled on top.

*CARB ALERT: One serving equals 18 carbohydrate grams.

RESOURCES

Products and Books

As a convenience for my readers and clients, Uni Key Health Systems has been the main distributor of my products, books, and services over the years. It carries Barlean's Essential Woman, the flax oil and evening primrose oil I helped formulate, as well as the vital fat-zapping supplements mentioned in this book, including the copper-free Female Multiple, iron-free Male Multiple, Weight-Loss Formula, CLA, H3 Plus, Super MaxEPA, black currant seed oil, and evening primrose oil. Call for a catalog of all the latest products. You may also order all of my books through Uni Key.

Uni Key Health Systems
P.O. Box 7168
Bozeman, MT 59771
1-800-888-4353
www.unikeyhealth.com

Additional Helpful Information

On the Web

www.annlouise.com If you would like to read my recent articles that have appeared in a variety of national publications, see a listing of all my books, or obtain a schedule of my upcoming events, just hop on the Internet and visit my Web site.

www.frenchmeadow.com This company offers good-tasting and nutritious organic breads that are cholesterol free, yeast free, dairy free, oil free, and sweetener free, with low sodium. Its Healthseed spelt bread is rich in omega 3s and 6s. It's also high in protein and fiber and made with flax, pumpkin, and sunflower seeds as well as sprouted legumes and grains.

www.flaxcouncil.ca This is a practical guide from the Flax Council of Canada, containing general and specialized flax facts. You will even find some great flax recipes.

www.fatsforhealth.com This is a comprehensive online guide for essential fatty acid information and news. You can get up-to-date data, articles, and news about EFAs in health, nutrition, beauty, disease treatment, and even pet care.

www.nutrinews.com Get the latest news and immediate help on health concerns, diet, supplements, and fitness as well as lifestyle needs and goals. This journalistic nutrition Web site even has calculators to track calorie-burning activities and your body's fat/lean composition, plus a food and recipe database, giving you the nutritional specifics of each.

Contacting Me

I really enjoy hearing from all my readers. Please feel free to e-mail me at gittleman@mindspring.com.

Partners for Women's Health

Key to Health Foundation
P.O. Box 882
Bozeman, MT 59771
(406) 585-9892
e-mail: gittleman@mindspring.com

Dedicating my career to women's health has been tremendously rewarding. But I wanted to help women even more, so I began searching for a venue to accomplish that deep-seated desire. I knew that if women partnered together, we could promote our health to even higher levels. That belief prompted me to create a nonprofit organization called Key to Health.

The Key to Health Foundation is committed to bettering women's health by creating a platform that will empower them at every transition of their lives, setting a nutrition revolution in motion that will reach out to future generations as well. To achieve this goal, Key to Health partners with other organizations that parallel its mission, principles, and holistic philosophy. It is through these combined, dedicated efforts that Key to Health plans to one day fund research studies for breakthrough natural remedies, responding to twenty-first-century health challenges. By supporting such endeavors, the keys to healing, longevity, and well-being will be readily available to women of every age.

If you would like to learn more about Key to Health or how you can become a partner in my quest to promote women's health, please write or e-mail me for an introductory packet.

BIBLIOGRAPHY

American Dietetic Association, Dietitians in general practice. Exchange Lists for Weight Management. Chicago, Ill., 1995.

Ando, H., et al. "Linoleic Acid and Alpha-Linolenic Acid Lighten Ultraviolet-Induced Hyperpigmentation of the Skin." *Archives of Dermatological Research* 290, no. 7 (July 1998): 375–81.

Andreassi, M., et al. "Efficacy of Gamma Linolenic Acid in the Treatment of Patients with Atopic Dermatitis." *The Journal of International Medical Research* 25 (1997): 266–74.

Bailey, Herbert. *Will It Keep You Young Longer?* New York: Bantam, 1980.

Belch, J. J., et al. "Effects of Altering Dietary Essential Fatty Acids on Requirements for Nonsteroidal Anti-Inflammatory Drugs in Patients with Rheumatoid Arthritis: A Double-Blind Placebo-Controlled Study." *Annals of Rheumatoid Disease* 47 (1988): 96–104.

Beutler, Jade. *Flax for Life: 101 Delicious Recipes and Tips Featuring Fabulous Flax Oil.* Encinitas, Calif.: Progressive Health Publishing, 1996.

Charmock, J. S., et al. "Gamma Linolenic Acid, Black Currant Seed and Evening Primrose Oil in the Prevention of Cardiac Arrhythmia in Aged Rats." *Nutritional Research* 14 (1994): 1089–99.

Colquhoun, I., and S. Bunday. "A Lack of Essential Fatty Acids as a Possible Cause for Hyperactivity in Children." *Medical Hypotheses* 7, (1981): 673–79.

Das, U. N., N. Madhavi, K. G. Sravan, M. Padma, and P. Sangeetha. "Can Tumor Cell Drug Resistance Be Reversed by Essential Fatty Acids and Their Metabolites?" *Prostaglandins leukot Essential Fatty Acids* 58 (1998): 39–54.

Deferne, J. L. "Resting Blood Pressure and Cardiovascular Reactivity to Mental Arithmetic in Mild Hypertensive Males Supplemented with Black Currant Seed Oil." *Journal of Human Hypertension* 10 (1996): 531–37.

Dreher, M. L., C. V. Maher, and P. Kearney. "The Traditional and Emerging Role of Nuts in Healthful Diets." *Nutrition Reviews* 54 (1996): 241–45.

Flax Council of Canada. *Flax, Family Favorites—Recipes and Healthful Tips.* Winnepeg, MB, Canada., 1999.

Fraser, G. E., et al. "A Possible Protective Effect of Nut Consumption on Risk of Coronary Heart Disease." *Archives of Internal Medicine* 152 (1992): 1416–24.

Gittleman, Ann Louise. *Beyond Pritikin.* New York: Bantam Books, 1996.

———. *Eat Fat, Lose Weight.* Los Angeles: Keats Publishing, 1999.

———. *Super Nutrition for Menopause.* Garden City Park, N.Y.: Avery, 1998.

Henz, B.M. "Double-Blind, Multicenter Analysis of the Efficacy of Borage Oil in Patients with Atopic Eczema." *British Journal of Dermatology* 140 (1999): 685–88.

Horrobin, D. F. "The Effects of Gamma Linolenic Acid on Breast Pain and Diabetic Neuropathy: Possible Noneicosanoid Mechanisms." *Prostaglandins leukot Essential Fatty Acids* 48 (1993): 101–104.

Ishikawa, Toshitsugu, et al. "Effects of Gamma Linolenic Acid on Plasma Lipoproteins and Apolipoproteins." *Atherosclerosis* 75 (1989): 95–104.

Levanthal, L. J., et al. "Treatment of Rheumatoid Arthritis with Gamma Linolenic Acid." *Annal of Internal Medicine* 119 (1993): 867–73.

Mayser, P., et al. "Omega 3 Fatty Acid-Based Lipid Infusion in Patients with Chronic Plaque Psoriasis: Results of a Double-Blind, Random-ized, Placebo-Controlled, Multicenter Trial." *Journal of American Academic Dermatology* 38 (1998): 539–47.

Neuringer, M., and W. E. Conner. "M-3 Fatty Acids in the Brain and Retina: Evidence for Their Essentiality." *Nutrition Reviews* 44 (1985): 285–94.

Norman, Jill. *Nuts.* New York: Bantam Books, 1990.

Pariza, M., et al. "Conjugated Linolenic Acid (GLA) Reduces Body Fat." *Experimental Biology Conference,* Abstract (1996).

———. "Conjugated Linoleic Acid (GLA) Reduces Body Fat." *FASEB Journal* 10, no. 3 (1996): A560.

Pariza, M.W., Y. Park, and M. E. Cook. "Mechanisms of Action of Conjugated Linoleic Acid: Evidence and Speculation." *Proceedings of the Society of Experimental Biological Medicine* 223 (2000): 8–13.

Prineas, R. J., et al. "Walnuts and Serum Lipids." *New England Journal of Medicine* 359 (1993): 329.

Sabate, J., and D. G. Hook. "Almonds, Walnuts, and Serum Lipids." In Spiller, G. A., ed., *Handbook of Lipids in Human Nutrition.* Boca Raton, Fla.: CRC Press, 1996, pp. 137–44.

Sabate, J., and G. E. Fraser. "The Probable Role of Nuts in Preventing Coronary Heart Disease." *Primary Care* 19 (1993): 65–72.

Sabate, J., et al. "Effects of Walnuts on Serum Lipid Levels and Blood Pressure in Normal Men." *New England Journal of Medicine* 328 (1993): 603–607.

Shils, M. E., J. A. Olson, M. Shike, and A. C. Ross. *Modern Nutrition in Health and Disease,* 9th edition. Baltimore, Md.: Williams and Wilkins, 1999, pp. 90–92, 1377–78.

Simopoulos, Artemis P. "Omega 3 Fatty Acids in Health and Disease and in Growth and Development." *The American Journal of Clinical Nutrition* 54 (1991): 438–63.

Simopoulos, Artemis P., and Jo Robinson. *The Omega Plan.* New York: Harper Collins, 1998.

Spiller, G. A., et al. "Nuts and Plasma Lipids: An Almond-Based Diet Lowers LDL-C While Preserving HDL-C." *Journal of American College of Nutrition* 17 (1998): 285–90.

Werbach, M. R. *Nutritional Influence on Illness,* 2d edition. Tarzana, Calif.: Third Line Press, 1993, pp. 13–22, 655–71.

Willet, W. C. "Diet and Health: What Should We Eat?" *Science* 264 (1994): 523–37.

Willet, W. C., et al. "Intake of Trans-Fatty Acids and Risk of Coronary Heart Disease Among Women." *The Lancet* 341 (1993): 581–85.

Zurier, R. B., P. DeLuca, and D. Rothman. "Gamma Linolenic Acid, Inflammation, Immune Responses, and Rheumatoid Arthritis." Y-S. Huang and D. E. Mills, eds., In *Gamma Linolenic Acid: Metabolism and Its Role in Nutrition and Medicine*. Champaign, Ill.: AOCS Press, 1996, pp. 129–136.

Zurier, R. B., et al. "Gamma Linolenic Acid Treatments of Rheumatoid Arthritis: A Randomized Placebo-Controlled Trial." *Arthritis Rheumatology* 30, no. 11 (1996): 1808–17.

INDEX